D0065482

THE
CONFUSION
ROOM

Also by Derek Tangye

The Minack Chronicles
A GULL ON THE ROOF
A CAT IN THE WINDOW
A DRAKE AT THE DOOR
A DONKEY IN THE MEADOW
LAMA
THE WAY TO MINACK
A CORNISH SUMMER
COTTAGE ON A CLIFF
A CAT AFFAIR
SUN ON THE LINTEL
SOMEWHERE A CAT IS WAITING (*Omnibus*)
THE WINDING LANE
WHEN THE WINDS BLOW
THE AMBROSE ROCK
A QUIET YEAR
THE CHERRY TREE
JEANNIE
THE EVENING GULL
THE WORLD OF MINACK (*illustrated anthology*)
MONTY'S LEAP
THE STORY OF THE MINACK CHRONICLES (*Omnibus*)

TIME WAS MINE
ONE KING
WENT THE DAY WELL (*editor*)

THE CONFUSION ROOM

Derek Tangye

MICHAEL JOSEPH

LONDON

To Cherry

MICHAEL JOSEPH LTD
Published by the Penguin Group
27 Wrights Lane, London W8 5TZ
Viking Penguin Inc., 375 Hudson Street, New York, New York 10014, USA
Penguin Books Australia Ltd, Ringwood, Victoria, Australia
Penguin Books Canada Ltd, 10 Alcorn Avenue, Toronto, Ontario, Canada M4V 3B2
Penguin Books (NZ) Ltd, 182–190 Wairau Road, Auckland 10, New Zealand

Penguin Books Ltd, Registered Offices: Harmondsworth, Middlesex, England

First published 1996
1 3 5 7 9 10 8 6 4 2

Set in 11.5/16pt Monophoto Imprint
Typeset by Datix International Limited, Bungay, Suffolk
Printed in England by Clays Ltd, St Ives plc

A CIP catalogue record for this book is available from the British Library

ISBN 0 7181 3972 0

The moral right of the author has been asserted

LIST OF ILLUSTRATIONS

I

I will begin exploring the Confusion Room today.

I intended to begin last week, last month, last year, the year before that. I talked about exploring the Confusion Room, but I did nothing. I was mesmerized by the task involved. The room contains the record of so much of our lives, the lives of Jeannie and myself. We dumped into the Confusion Room every written item, and much else, which we thought we ought to keep.

'If you were run over by a bus,' a friend said, 'who is going to unravel it all?'

When Jeannie died, I was able to look after her secrets, censor them, burn them, cherish those items which were not secrets. That is what you can do if you are the one who is left. You are in charge. There is no stranger prying into the personal past.

'If you were run over by a bus . . .'

It was a pungent remark. Who could unravel it all? It is hard enough organizing a removal from one house to another. What do we keep? Shall that piece of furniture fit into the new home? Yes . . . no . . . It has sentimental value and on that score we should keep it, but it is too large and it really has no place. And what shall we do with the books? Such questions may be difficult to answer, but they are nothing to those which have to be answered if you are run over by a bus.

That remark, therefore, set me ruminating. I am unable to keep under control the paraphernalia of my life in any case. Files litter the cottage with scrawled messages on the front covers: 'Letters to answer', 'Possible material for a book', 'Odds and ends but worth looking through again', 'Newspaper cuttings which might be useful', and there is the inevitable 'To file'. The latter is a menace. It bulges with letters which I aim to set out in order, name and address of the senders written on the front of more files. Letters from readers, for instance, which I can quickly refer to when necessary. Such letters provide the push I so often need to get on with my work, and I look upon them as coming from friends though I may never have met the writers personally. I wrote in this connection the following:

The secret weapon of the book world is the close friendship which develops between the reader and the author of a sensitive book, an author who can belong to any period in time.

Yes, it is time to act. I will go down to the Confusion Room at once.

The Confusion Room was a stable when we first came to Minack, a stable used by a neighbouring farmer for his two horses. Small farmers did not have tractors in those days, and the horses used to lumber in the fields pulling the farm implements. I will always remember those horses because of the part they played one November morning when I had an accident.

I was rotovating a cliff meadow with my hand-held motorized rotovator while some distance away my neighbour and his horses were ploughing a field. I remember how, as I roared up and down the meadow, I kept glancing across at them, charmed by such a rustic scene. It was a costly glance. I suddenly lost my concentration, the rotovator hit a rock, leapt out of control, and one of the steel hooks caught my left foot and pierced it. The engine jammed and I was left pinioned on the ground, chained by the hook which held my foot as if it was on a butcher's hook. I could see the horses, and then saw the farmer leave them and begin racing towards me. I was on the verge of fainting when he arrived.

'All right, mate . . . lie still. I'll get the tractor off you.'

I was in bed for a fortnight, then on crutches, and hobbling with a stick for a further six weeks.

The farmer left that farm for a larger one and Jeannie and I took over the stable, and also the other half of the building, more ancient than the stable half, the ground layered with cobbles, odd signs of one-time feeding troughs, a rickety wooden plank attic where in days gone by potato seeds used to be painstakingly laid out in November, growing green shoots over Christmas time, then ready to be planted in the early cliff meadows in late January and early February. Primitive times, times that Jeannie and I were on the edge of and which gave us pleasure, the pleasure of living with reality, not theory ... and then the primitive times began gradually to fade away.

Yes, I would start exploring the Confusion Room today. I waited for the post to arrive, then sat on the sofa reading the letters, grateful to the senders for troubling to write, cogitated for a while, then forced myself to get up. This was Confusion Room day. Don't put it off. Let me start immediately.

I went to the porch door in a determined mood, opened it, and found Cherry waiting to come in. Cherry, heroine of *The Cherry Tree*, is my best friend. She understands me. She senses when I am in an emotional mood, needing a soothing influence. She will suddenly appear, whether I am indoors sitting at my desk or, maybe, I am on the patio called the bridge, staring out across Mount's Bay, pondering. She will nestle beside me. I will put out my hand, gently stroking her, talking to her, telling her what is on my mind. She is the cushion which receives my worries and my problems. I am safe with her. I tell her my secrets, knowing that they will go no further. I am trying to write, suffering from a blank mind, and she will jump beside my typewriter, pushing her head against the keys, seemingly trying to inspire me. The bond between us is so close that in the years we have been alone together we have been separated for only a total of three weeks. She is my anchor, my source of motivation. Motivation of love.

She gave me a silent miaow, as Paul Gallico would

have said; and I knew that I had to retreat to the galley of a kitchen, open a tin for her and give her some milk, I was aware that by the time I had achieved such tasks my enthusiasm would be waning. I refused, however, to succumb. I provided Cherry with a portion out of the tin and a saucer of milk, and was delighted that my conscience was now free. I could continue my way to the Confusion Room.

I shut the door, leaving a window in the porch ajar so that Cherry could jump outside if she so wished, and walked the few steps to the water butt which stands at the corner of the cottage. There one turns left down the path, then along a short part of the lane to the stable building and the Confusion Room.

I turned the corner and there was a hullabaloo above me. Maddeningly, the Lager Louts had arrived to interrupt my good intentions. The Lager Louts, two gulls so called because of their raucous behaviour, have haunted Minack for some while. One of them had never grown up, had remained perpetually juvenile, maintaining a noisy squeak like the sound of an instrument needing oil. The other, besides its squawks, would bang with its beak on the porch glass roof, bang, bang, bang, until I surrendered, left whatever I was doing and threw up slices of bread.

I do not have the affection for the Lager Louts that I have for the evening gull. The evening gull is silent, too silent as he arrives as dusk is falling. I wish he would make some sound, give some message telling me of his arrival. I would not then, from time to time,

5

have a terrible guilty feeling that I have forgotten him, have sat instead with a drink in my hand, Cherry on my lap, musing while the evening gull sat above me on the roof too polite to demand my attention. Only as he leaves to fly back to the cliffs and the sea am I made aware of his waiting presence. As he flies away, he gives out a disgruntled chuckle.

I reached the Confusion Room door, fumbled the key into the padlock, opened it . . . and at the same moment became aware of the donkeys, massive brown Merlin, tiny grey Susie, snorting at me over the stone wall at the edge of the stable building a couple of yards away. Once again my good intentions were arrested. I had to turn back and go to the Volvo which I use as a kind of spare larder and in which were the packets of Rich Tea biscuits which provide the donkeys with much pleasure. I returned with a packet, quietened the snorts and then at last entered the Confusion Room.

I never let anyone into the Confusion Room, no stranger that is. A stranger would assess my character as being insecure, illogical and possessing no sense of method. No wonder. The stranger would see the jumble of boxes, suitcases, instruments like a chainsaw, a metal detector, out-of-date radios, clothes like old shirts and trousers, a discarded mattress, masses of books, gramophone records, paintings we had collected over the years, a filing cabinet containing letters from readers, letters since the first of the Minack Chronicles was written, letters which have enriched our lives.

I stood at the open door. On my left, wedged

between the wall and the filing cabinet, was the orange tablecloth which we had attached to a post when the *QE 2* came to Minack. Captain Warwick, then captain of the liner, had written to say he enjoyed the Minack story and would like to visit us, but would have to bring the *QE 2* along with him . . . And so he did, sailing a mile offshore, the donkeys, Penny and Fred at the time, hooting, the ship sounding its siren and the orange tablecloth waving a greeting in the breeze.

Alongside the wall on my right a carpenter had built a wardrobe with sliding doors, thirty feet long and ten feet high with a space between the top and the ceiling where the suitcases harbouring many of our records were stored. We had the wardrobe built in a moment of panic. George Brown, a man without personal ambition, a great Labour politician of his period, too ebullient for some, a man of unadulterated integrity, had written asking if he and his wife could spend a few days with us. He had recently resigned from being Foreign Secretary and he wanted a retreat away from the attentions of the press, but he was still Deputy Leader of the Labour Party. The prospect of their arrival was alarming. Where would they stay? We had our bedroom, the sitting room, the spare room which was bought as a chickenhouse and the bathroom. Where would they put their clothes? Hence the wardrobe in the Confusion Room. Jeannie and I would give over the cottage to George and Sophie, and we would sleep in the Confusion Room. The wardrobe would contain our clothes. It proved to be a lucky moment of panic.

The wardrobe became the base for many of our clothes. Those of Jeannie are still there.

Opposite me across the Confusion Room was an in-depth ledge beneath the widow facing out to sea. Upon this ledge was a heap of empty tobacco tins. I have no explanation as to why I have left them there over the years, but they represent the hours of endeavour in writing the Chronicles. A blank mind, not an idea in my head as to how I can begin the next paragraph, sitting there in front of the typewriter, staring at a blank page. Then a flash of hope! Let me fill a pipe with Down the Road Tobacco.

My brother Nigel had persuaded me to be a pipe smoker. He was an aeronautical adviser at the time, and his office was in Half Moon Street off Piccadilly; and at the corner of Piccadilly and Half Moon Street was an exclusive tobacconist called Freeman's. It was Mr Freeman, the owner, who introduced me to the tobacco mixture known as Down the Road and I have used it ever since.

Incidentally, I took Jeannie to see Mr Freeman soon after we had met. 'Useful,' I said to her with effrontery, 'to know your boyfriend's favourite tobacconist.' In due course Freeman's sold to Simmons of the Burlington Arcade and Simmons sold to Dunhill. And why call it Down the Road? One of the early customers had a coach and four, and once he wrote to the original supplier saying: 'Whenever I start off down the road I'm smoking a pipe with your tobacco.'

There is a wooden beam which spans the Confusion

Room from one wall to the other, and on it are cards representing our victories at the Penzance Flower Show, the earliest flower show in the country after that of the Scilly Isles. It was a very prestigious show at the time of our victories, and as I stood looking at the cards I remembered the most important ones. First for a box of wallflowers, first for a mixed box of spring flowers, first for a box of overwintered lettuces . . .

We had pasted the cards on the beam because the Confusion Room was at the time the setting for our flower bunching. It was a special kind of bunching. Daffodils were bunched elsewhere, but in the Confusion Room we did the Cornish posies, an idea we had thought up ourselves. They consisted of spring flowers, those that were flowering in late February and early March, some under glass: forget-me-nots, wallflowers, calendula, freesia, miniature daffodils, violets, anemones, and perhaps sprigs of veronica. Our salesman in Covent Garden was enthusiastic about them, and for two seasons the hard work they required always fetched for us a good price. Then began the copiers, the price fell and our enthusiasm for Cornish posies faded away.

One morning I had carried in two baskets of wallflowers and had begun to peel away the leaves when the postman arrived with a telegram. Jeannie was at the bench, Jane and Shelagh, our teenage helpers, beside her, bunching the posies, placing each one in a jam jar when it had been completed. These three had such pleasure in the work they were doing, full of

9

concentration only broken by silly remarks to bring levity to their task. 'Two hundred and sixty days to Christmas,' Shelagh would say. The postman handed me the telegram and I opened it, only to find it was meant for Jeannie. It was from the BBC.

There was currently a television serial based on Arnold Bennett's *Imperial Palace*, which in its turn had been based on the Savoy Hotel in London. The telegram invited Jeannie to comment on the serial on a special programme which was scheduled within three days. She had been invited because of her book, which is now a classic, called *Meet Me at the Savoy*, her story of her time with the Savoy Group where she was described by a Hollywood columnist as 'the prettiest publicity girl in the world'.

Jeannie remonstrated. She never sought publicity for herself. She believed in being natural and, in contrast to the organized publicity for the famous who came her way, she herself had a different philosophy. She believed that genuine publicity came naturally, a nudge here or there, of course, but not artificially arranged. She did not want to take up the BBC's offer and said she preferred to continue bunching Cornish posies.

Within twenty-four hours, however, she had surrendered her basic way of life, the crouching along beds of daffodils picking at speed, the Cornish posies, the early morning with the wind in her hair (Carol Gibbons would break away from whatever tune he was playing when he saw her coming down the steps into the

Savoy Restaurant and begin playing the Stephen Foster song 'I Dream of Jeannie with the Light Brown Hair'), and she had become again the sophisticated girl, treated as a star, with a suite overlooking the Thames on the fourth floor of the Savoy with a view that Charlie Chaplin described as the most romantic city view in the world.

I was there, too, in modest attendance. A car drove us to Television Centre. Jeannie had had a preview of the programme, and she had been professionally disapproving of one scene in which the actor who was playing the hotel manager was seen holding a cigarette in his hand while receiving hotel guests. She decided to make a special point about this in her introductory remarks. All was ready for her to do so, the camera focussed upon her, the programme about to begin . . . and she began to hiccup. A nightmare moment for Jeannie. I watched with horror, but when the cameras began to turn her will power had won. She was brilliant. The next day we were in the Savoy lift, and I heard a young woman say to a young man, 'Did you see that very pretty girl talking about hotels on TV last night? I thought her fascinating.' Jeannie hid her face.

I stood looking around the Confusion Room, not with a sense of nostalgia but with one of inquisitiveness. What snatches of the past might I suddenly find that might explain my attitudes to the present? And where should I begin to look? Labour Warms was the answer to such a question.

Labour Warms was a feature of my nursery at my

family home of Glendorgal overlooking Porth Bay near Newquay. I loved that home when I was a child as I now love Minack. It absorbed my whole youthful being, and during my school holidays I would never leave the grounds except to play golf at Fistral Bay.

Labour Warms is a massive cupboard made of teak. The top half has two open trays, the bottom half three solid drawers and a miniature cupboard. The significance of Labour Warms, however, lies in the impact on my juvenile mind of the slogan which in blue letters stood out across the top of the cupboard. The slogan was often pointed out to me.

LABOUR WARMS SLOTH HARMS.

And it still stares at me.

There is a file in one of the drawers of letters I wrote to my mother which I retrieved after she died. There is a quantity of other letters, angry, enthusiastic, puzzled letters; long-ago newspaper extracts; diaries of my time at Harrow School and of my youthful days when I was setting out to learn about life, greedily trying to gain from the experiences of those I met, by reading books by authors who wrote because of their passion for everyday life and its vagaries, and not because of television serial temptations.

There are scrawled pages in these diaries where I castigate myself for my inferiority complex, for my chronic obsession that I was a failure in everything I tried to do . . . pages about my shyness with a girl, my nervous, fumbling approach . . . and then a sudden buoyant page of hope, of excitement that the years lay ahead and I had plenty of time ... then a page of frustration in that I had no motivation except a vague one that I wanted to be someone who could rejoice that he had had a full life. All the perennial complexities of youth, varied in their nature but always fundamentally the same throughout the ages. True values never change, only fashion values change. Infant children still excitedly wait for Father Christmas to leave a present at the bottom of the bed.

I gazed at the slogan LABOUR WARMS SLOTH HARMS. How strange that the little boy looked up at it in innocence. All the years had gone by with his learning, his failings, sudden successes, new loves, passing loves, Jeannie's love, adventures, distant travels, unpleasant situations, so much happiness, moments of despair. Here I was in the Confusion Room surrounded by the evidence of my life and in the mood to begin collecting it when I heard a car coming down the lane. It hesitated at Monty's Leap, then revved up towards the cottage, passing the Confusion Room's open door.

It was an unmarked police car, and I recognized the occupants. They were two CID officers with whom I had been in touch before, since before Christmas.

II

One Saturday before Christmas, Steve from Camborne, who comes to Minack from time to time to deal with the heavy work, took a stroll around Minack cliffs after his work had been completed.

'Happy Christmas!' I said as he set off.

I went back to the cottage, not expecting to see him again, and settled down to read the Christmas cards which had arrived by the morning post. Cherry saw me looking comfortable, proceeded to jump on my lap and pinioned me into immobility as is the custom of cats who wish to assert their authority. I was thus sitting on the sofa, the sofa which has followed me from home to home since I first had a home of my own in Elm Park Garden Mews off the King's Road in Chelsea, when, half an hour later, there was a knock on the porch door and the voice of Steve asked to come in.

'What's happened?' I asked, puzzled since I had not expected to see him again that day.

Steve did not tell his tale dramatically. He simply gave the facts . . . but first I had better set the scene in geographical and emotional terms.

Minack is divided into two halves. Our cottage with twenty acres is rented, and on the other side of the valley there are a further twenty acres which we were able to buy. It was land which we had looked out upon over the years, and we wanted it to remain an example of the true Cornwall for ever, a natural haven for wild creatures and for those who are seeking peace of mind.

At the entrance to this land, alongside the wooden gate is a plaque, white letters on dark green, saying:

THE DEREK AND JEANNIE TANGYE
MINACK CHRONICLES
NATURE RESERVE.
A PLACE FOR SOLITUDE.

We called this land Oliver land. Oliver was a black cat whom I wrote about in *When the Winds Blow*. Jeannie and I saw him first in the far corner of the large field in the land which, in due course, we were going to own. We were standing on the patio which we called the bridge, because it looks out on the moorland and the sea of Mount's Bay and it is as if one is standing on the bridge of a ship.

Suddenly we saw this black cat poised to pounce on some potential victim, and we watched its body swaying, holding back for a moment, then forward again . . . and the pounce! It missed.

The cat began to haunt Minack, and it disturbed us because Lama was with us then and reaching the end of her time – Lama who had come to us in a storm, belonging to nowhere, who had arrived after Monty of *A Cat in the Window* had died and I had sworn I would never have another cat unless an unknown one arrived at the door in a storm who was black . . . and Lama fulfilled my conditions.

15

Thus I had no intention of her home being infiltrated by another cat, upsetting her after all the years she had given us. So when Oliver began to infiltrate coming down the lane to Monty's Leap, sitting there staring up towards the cottage, waiting for the saucer which Jeannie, a chronic cat lover, was sure to leave for him, I myself, an original cat hater, used to shoo him away if he came closer. I would shout at him. I would make an angry noise with my feet on the gravel. I would try to frighten him. But he refused to be influenced. For some strange reason he had decided that Minack was the home he wanted, and so day after day we would see him in the lane undeterred by my threats. Then one day he played a trump card. One Sunday morning I was standing where the little stream known as Monty's Leap crosses the lane when, twenty yards ahead, I saw to my astonishment a little ginger kitten emerge from the undergrowth . . . and beside it was Oliver; and this kitten was to become Ambrose of *The Ambrose Rock*.

This land we had bought, this Oliver land, stretched in moorland fashion towards the ancient standing rock known as Carn Barges. Jeannie and I used to feel a nostalgic sweetness that the great rock, standing on its granite plinth where we once had stood staring across towards Minack cottage, sensing our future, feeling sure within ourselves that here lay our destiny, now belonged to us. It was a rich moment of our lives when on our first day of ownership we bent down and touched the earth, pledging that whatever happened

to either of us this land would forever belong to untamed Cornwall. It was then that the idea of the Minack
Chronicles Trust was born.

Here on Oliver land is the Ambrose Rock, named
after the little ginger kitten who had been christened
Ambrose by Jeannie, and who, when he was older, had
come with us on our first day of ownership, and had
suddenly leapt on the great granite rock and sat there
purring. This rock that had stood there for aeons of
time now became known as the Ambrose Rock.

It has become a magic rock which people touch and
have secret wishes, a rock which is an antidote to logic.
I remember Jeannie walking there from the cottage,
not telling me what she intended to do but it was at a
time when her very young nephew was gravely ill in
the Birmingham Children's Hospital. The same week
we had heard that a young girl who had visited us with
her mother was seriously ill in Great Ormond Street
Hospital in London. Jeannie had walked to the Ambrose Rock to touch it in order to inspire a miracle.
There was to be a miracle, two miracles. Both Jeannie's
nephew and the little girl thrived.

Our life at Minack, however, had begun with only
six acres, most of which was moorland. No sensible
person would have expected to make a living out of
such an uncultivated morass of bracken, gorse, thorn
bushes and brambles, but Jeannie and I were not sensible. We were so thankful to be released from the arti-
ficiality of our sophisticated life and the stresses it
had involved that we believed our enthusiasm could

achieve the impossible. And there was another reason for such optimism. Within these six acres was cliff land, and cliff land along this Cornish coast was famed for being the earliest growing area in the country. Daffodils and spring flowers were the first to be sent to market, new potatoes the first to appear in the shops in May. There was no competition from overseas, no aircraft shuttling produce from distant parts of the world. Cornish growers of cliff land had the early markets to themselves.

Our first task, therefore, was to set about opening up our cliff land, and as we began cutting away the undergrowth we found outlines of small meadows, small meadows which had been in cultivation decades before but which, for some long-ago reason, had been allowed to die out. The meadows were steep, falling down like stepping stones to the rocks and the sea. It was a beautiful setting. Jeannie and I would take a rest and sit on the ground, watching the gulls bobbing on the water, a cormorant drying its outstretched wings, a flock of gannets passing swiftly a mile offshore, cargo ships spotting the distant horizon, and all the while we would be listening to the murmur of the sea. It was as if we belonged to the time when the meadows were last in cultivation, a time when countrymen looked at the sky and made their own weather forecasts, when the leaders of nations had time to think quietly, no aircraft to rush them hither and thither, no weaving blocks of television cameramen watching their every move, no tabloid newspapers disclosing their very private lives, no fringe members of the Royal Family publicly playing the 'tell-all' role for the world to read. It was a time when there were standards to observe. One such standard was to avoid moaning about your partner, even to a neighbour.

We were wonderfully free, enjoying a freedom we could not have experienced if we had begun our adventure today. Now facts and figures produced by accountants would have proved us lunatics. Of course some of our friends thought us lunatics in any case. They were caught inside their conventional lives. They could not understand the joy we had in slashing the ancient meadows open again. Occasionally Jeannie, so deliciously pretty, would break off from the work and run naked down to the rocks and the pool which awaited her swim. We were living the freedom which the human race chases.

As the years went by our minds became more and more involved in the mystique of the Minack cliff. We would walk away from the cottage, isolated as it was from the fractious activity and noise of modern civilization, yet arrive at the cliff meadows and find ourselves in another world. It was as if a spiritual cloak, born at the beginning of time, enveloped us. Here was tranquillity. No artificial stresses to upset it. No human being watching. No evil actions to threaten us. Nature was in charge.

At the beginning we were strangers. It is impossible to get immediate acceptance from a piece of land one has acquired. One has to inch one's way into it and be part of the traumas, the wonder, the excitement of it. It is a form of education, and as the years went by Jeannie and I had such an education.

We began our education with early potatoes, Sharpe's Express and the Duke of York, which had the flavour of truly new potatoes but are now out of favour because the market requires size not flavour. We caressed our new potatoes, carefully avoiding any cut in them as we shovelled them out of the ground. Then came the artistic side of growing new potatoes. We dropped each one into what was called a chip, which held fourteen pounds of potatoes, lining the bottom with potato leaves and topping up the chip with more leaves. Then we carried the chips up the cliff, two at a time, and on reaching the top we would weigh them and tie them up, and rejoice sometimes that so many chips had been dug in a day. Above all we felt pride in the quality of our new potatoes.

Growing potatoes cleaned the ground, eradicating the harsh undergrowth roots, and we began to plant daffodil bulbs in many of the meadows. We planted, for the most part, the variety called Magnificence, a beautiful deep yellow, very early daffodil with a soft scent. Around Christmas time, after the green shoots had appeared and they were several inches high, we used to have fun testing the base of the shoots for buds. There was, however, a serious side to such fun for we were trying to ascertain what kind of daffodil season lay ahead. If we found lots of buds were forming, we knew a good season lay ahead. At other times we would groan to each other that there seemed to be hardly any buds. 'Oh dear,' I would say to Jeannie, 'I'm afraid it is going to be a very light crop.'

We had a favourite meadow, high up the cliff, where we grew Magnificence. The meadow was bordered by undergrowth and was very secret, with no possibility, it seemed, of any person finding it. Jeannie and I would often sit there, at any time of the year, musing about life or just being silent, staring out to sea. At one time, before Oliver land became ours, we thought it would be the perfect peaceful place for our ashes. 'A long time before that will happen,' I used to say cheerfully.

After Jeannie died I stopped working the cliff because it was no longer profitable with horticultural produce from all over the world being flown into the markets. Nature began to take over the meadows, leaving the daffodils in the spring to peer up into the jungle above them. I felt sad that our cliff days were over and that the cliff was again as we first saw it, but at least I could be happy to know that I was returning it to its natural purity. No man-made pollution.

I was wrong in thinking this.

Steve had come to tell me why. I wrote in *Monty's Leap*:

He had gone for a walk . . . towards Carn Barges. On the way, however, he noticed at the bottom of our field a faint track which might have been a badger's track, leading from the coastal path along the top of our one-time cliff meadows.

'I had an instinct to follow it,' he said. 'Perhaps it is because I am a countryman that I sensed something.'

The track, he explained, was so slight that strands of brambles covered it at places, and at one spot he had to crawl on hands and knees beneath a huge bramble bush. I realized that the spot he described was by the gate which led down steps (all now covered by undergrowth) to the cliff meadows, and eventually to the rocks and pools where we used to bathe. He pressed on and, about fifty yards further, he found an opening down a steep bank.

When he reached the bottom of the steep bank, he came up against the massive undergrowth falling down to the rocks and he could go no further. Then suddenly to his right he saw a gap, and through the gap he saw what seemed to be a cultivated small meadow. He pushed his way through the gap and, sure enough, there was this meadow of newly turned earth, and just below it, another such meadow of newly turned earth. From his description I guessed they were the two small meadows where we grew Magnificence daffodils [and which] were very special to us.

The following morning I investigated. When I reached the meadows and saw the way they had been dug (no sign of our beloved Magnificence, which should have been shooting green by now but which had obviously been taken away and planted elsewhere), I realized that a professional cliff man must have been at work. But who? And what was his purpose? When was the work done? Implements had to be carried there. Who would have known such meadows existed? Who would have thought it worth the hard work and risk? And for what reason?

I remember how I had in those first hours, some foolish explanations. Perhaps, for instance, it was an IRA dump. It had recently been reported that the IRA had such coastal dumps in Wales; and indeed it was this fantasy suspicion that prompted me to report the situation to the police, and the two CID officers who had just passed the Confusion Room door had been the first to investigate the matter.

I had directed them to the meadows; and they had returned holding up a dead plant.

'What's that?' I had asked.

'Cannabis,' one of them replied.

'What do you mean?'

'Cannabis has been grown down your cliff, and the meadows are now being prepared for this year's crop.'

Cannabis instead of daffodils in the cliff meadows that Jeannie and I had nurtured and loved.

III

Rain began to fall as the CID officers emerged from their car. I led them up the path to the porch, disturbing Cherry who was curled on the red check tablecloth. I sat down on one side of the table, and the two men opposite me.

'Have you any idea who might be doing this?' asked one of them. 'The meadows are very hidden. The person concerned must have an intimate knowledge of your land.'

Cherry had jumped off the table and gone to the door, wanting to be let out. 'It's raining, Cherry. You won't like it,' I said, keeping the door shut. 'Frankly,' I went on to the CID men, 'I haven't a clue. What puzzles me is that cliff work needs a specialist. Cliff meadows are not like an ordinary garden. They are very steep, and everything has to be done by hand, slow work and exhausting, first hacking the ground to clean it with a long-handled fork, then turning the ground with a long-handled shovel. Nothing like that has been done since Jeannie died, and the man who helped us has long given up such work. He remains an incorruptible friend.'

'Have you talked to him about what has happened?'

'Not yet.'

24

Cliff workers no longer exist. Cliff meadows sheltered from the winds, facing the morning sun that glitters the sea of Mount's Bay, used to be cherished by those who had them. Here grew the early potatoes, the early daffodils which reached the markets before the fields were harvested, thus fetching high prices. But modern methods of growing have destroyed this advantage, and the cliff meadows have disappeared from use; and thus, along this beautiful natural stretch of the Cornish coast, they have been buried in undergrowth.

'Your friend,' said the officer, 'might be able to help. In a small region like this he will have known his fellow cliff workers, the ones who worked in those times. Perhaps you could ask him to make a list of them.'

'I'll do so.'

Then I added: 'I feel I ought to tell you that I am not so concerned about the actual growing of the cannabis. What has enraged me is that anyone should steal the use of my land, steal the daffodils we had planted ourselves, steal the dreams of Jeannie and myself and, for that matter, putting me at risk with the law. If a stranger had discovered the cannabis, would not suspicion have fallen on me? Cannabis being grown on *my* meadows, and so hidden?'

At that moment a drip of water from the rain-spattered glass roof fell on the head of one of the officers.

'Oh, I do apologize,' I said. 'If you move a little to the left, it ought to be all right.'

The porch, the original porch, was built for us by a craftsman called Ken Semmens. Ken was very conscientious, and it took a very long time before the porch was completed. Everything had to be perfect. The wood had to be treated as if it was gold, no section was put into place unless Ken was satisfied that it was in perfect condition. Alas, as the years went by, I failed to care for the wood as I should have done. Had I done so it would not have begun to rot, and we would have continued to have a porch which had no leaks. As it was I had to have the porch rebuilt. No craftsman was available. Machine-made frames were used. The glass did not fit. Leaks began immediately, and they have continued despite many efforts to check them.

'I'll fetch you an umbrella,' I have said to many a visitor. They always laugh.

The officer had been unperturbed. His mind was upon what I had said to him.

'We appreciate your point of view,' he began, 'but growing cannabis is against the law, and therefore our task is to catch the culprit. Once we have done that we can add further charges like theft and trespass.'

I have never been interested in experimenting with drugs. I did not belong to a generation that did so, although I remember a willowy lady called Brenda Dean Paul who lived near me in Chelsea and who achieved notoriety from her drug addiction and her arrests; and I remember I used to look at her with a kind of innocent awe. What sort of strange devil possessed her? And then I found myself reflecting what sort of devil possessed me when I drank too much whisky? Where was the difference?

There was, however, an occasion when I once smoked opium. I was a clerk in Unilever at the time, acting as a tea boy for junior managers during the day and being a deb's delight at night ('deb's delight' was a term used to describe young men who were on the permanent invitation list for débutante parties).

At one such party I met a wealthy South American diplomat who invited me and another young man to have dinner with him at his palatial apartment in Eaton Square. When dinner was over he suggested a pipe of opium, and the three of us adjourned to another room where the paraphernalia of opium smoking was produced. In due course there I was puffing away like any old Chinaman.

After a while I said: 'I don't feel any effects.'

'Nor do I,' said my companion.

'Ah,' said the wealthy diplomat, 'you must come here often. Get the habit. Life will become beautiful.'

I now had a question to ask the officers, a question I could not ask the staff of the Ministry of Agriculture's local office.

'How does one grow cannabis?'

It sounded simple. It was like growing early potatoes but staggeringly more profitable. An early potato plant might produce enough tender potatoes to earn a pound. A cannabis plant growing five feet tall like a tomato plant could earn from its leaves at least a hundred pounds when harvested; and they had to be planted only eighteen inches apart.

'In the present case,' said one of the officers, 'they

have already got the ground ready, sown the fertilizer, and have circled the meadows with wire netting.'

'To stop the rabbits becoming drug addicts?'

'That's it,' said the officer, smiling. Then he went on, 'The plants are now being grown secretly in a greenhouse and they will be planted out in March. Then they will be given the usual looking after, weeding and so on, until late July or August when the harvesting takes place.' And he added, 'We're in the first week of January. We have got eight months in which to catch the culprit.'

'What do you want me to do?'

'We have our own ways of investigating, but you can watch for any strangers on the coastal path from Carn Barges.'

'There will obviously be strangers walking there.'

'Strangers at unusual hours, in the evenings or early morning.'

'But supposing the culprit is coming from the other way, from the Land's End direction? It is impossible to see anyone from the cottage.'

'Well,' said the officer, 'if we can't trace anyone coming up from Lamorna and past Carn Barges, it will narrow our enquiries.'

I had had experience of this kind of investigation. I was for a while a crime correspondent of a national newspaper, and I was for eleven years a member of MI5. I was aware of the pitfalls. I knew how a line of enquiry could lead one into suspecting someone entirely innocent because of circumstantial evidence. I was aware, too, of the way an investigator can be deceived by the charm of the person he is investigating. I am aware of the skill of the confidence trickster, of the bravado of his manner, his self-control which prevents any slip of the tongue, and of his self-discipline which he maintains over a period of time.

In this category I think of the Soviet spies, Blunt, Philby, Burgess and Maclean. Of course they had to have luck in order to survive, and one form of the luck was never to be observed meeting their case officers. They had to meet in out of ordinary locations, and I have often wondered how I would have reacted if, by chance, I had entered a pub in some unlikely place and seen Blunt closeted with a strange man, a foreigner. Would I have innocently gone up to him? How would Blunt have reacted? Would I have reported my encounter the next day to my boss? Would he have thought the meeting was suspicious? I doubt it. MI5 was built around a class system which took it for granted that anyone who belonged to the class would never betray his country.

I used to meet Blunt regularly in connection with my work, and he would often ask for help with some enquiry, an enquiry which, only after Blunt's exposure, did I realize he was making on behalf of the KGB. Yet in retrospect I can recall no instance when he aroused any suspicion in my mind. I had, however, my doubts about Philby and Burgess, Philby in particular, but these doubts were only intuition. There was one occasion when I was in Philby's office discussing the recruitment of an English journalist to act as an agent in the Lisbon network which Philby ran. I can recall vividly his piercing eyes staring at me across his desk, and I had this intuitive feeling that the look was evil – and it was, of course. He was to use this innocent journalist on behalf of the KGB.

Then there are the conventional confidence tricksters who have deceived me. Perhaps I am gullible, perhaps it is because I want to believe people are sincere when we first meet, and I want to continue to believe it until with a shock I realize they are liars.

I have also been a confidence trickster, for a journalist is usually acting as one. I found, for instance, that I did not mind what I did in order to achieve the good story that my news editor set me out to pursue. The methods adopted in those days were not as deceitful as those used today. Hidden microphones were not used, and there were no long-distance cameras making privacy impossible. Nor was there the ruthless policy of bribery in order to obtain salacious stories. None the less a journalist had often to be a confidence trickster in order to keep his job. In the beginning my conscience was clear because I was so keen to obtain the story I had been sent out to gain that the ethics of my behaviour did not register in my mind. I would display such innocence, such sympathy, when I interviewed some unfortunate character that he would become confident in my sincerity and would yield to my manner, and I would get the story I was after. Gradually, though, disgust set in. Such disgust is inevitable after one has seen, time after time, the pain one has caused to the character concerned. Present-day journalism excuses such behaviour as in 'the public interest'. It is difficult to believe.

My confidence trickster role during one period was of a different nature. It was during the Hitler war. One of my MI5 jobs was to see the Secretary of the Cabinet once a week to inform him of the news behind the news, political gossip, rumours about well-known individuals, scandals, the general state of morale among the well-informed, I knew that anything of special importance would be on Churchill's desk within a few hours. Political plots against Churchill were rife at one period of the war, and many wanted him removed from power. He suffered what all Prime Ministers have to suffer at some time during their term of office.

One of the critics was Claud Cockburn, a Communist, who wrote for the *Daily Worker* under the name of Frank Pitcairn, and who also wrote a weekly broadsheet called *The Week*. He was a brilliant man, amazingly well-informed, a delightful companion, full of fun and mischief. He used to come to our Sunday lunches at Cholmondley House, Richmond, at which prominent figures of the international, political and journalistic world would be the guests, and over which Jeannie used to preside. Claud would mock Jeannie. 'When we Communists come to power,' he would say looking at Jeannie, 'you as a capitalist will be shot.' It made Jeannie laugh.

My chief at MI5 knew of my friendship with Claud, and he decided that I should make more use of it.

'I want you to act,' he said, 'as if you are a disillusioned member of MI5, that you are a potential traitor.'

31

I now set out to gain Claud's confidence by feed-ing him with apparently inside information about the activities of MI5, information which had been in-vented by my chief and which was calculated to intrigue Claud and increase my standing as a potential traitor – a fact, it was calculated, that he would pass on to his KGB contacts. I was therefore being groomed by my chief to be a double-agent, and as a consequence I began to act in a theatrical manner. I proceeded to behave in the traditional way of a spy, telling Claud that I feared my telephone was tapped and that when he rang me he must use a false name. Each new meeting place had to be agreed on at the previous meeting so it was never mentioned on the telephone.

This charade was carried on for several months, and it appeared to be going well. Claud became increas-ingly open with me and seemed confident that I was indeed a genuine disillusioned member of MI5. Then suddenly it was all over. I arrived at one of our sched-uled meetings (it was in a Soho pub), and Claud never appeared. Nor did he contact me afterwards. The link had been broken. It was a week or two later that I had an explanation. A contact of mine was in Claud's com-pany when my name came up.

'Tangye?' snorted Claud, 'I wouldn't trust him fur-ther than I can kick a grand piano!'

Who had given my role away? Was it Blunt? He was an aide to my chief.

The CID officers were preparing to leave. It had

stopped raining. The two gulls, the Lager Louts, were up on the roof squawking their raucous cries, demanding bread. Cherry was still at the door waiting to be let out.

'Ring us at the police station if you have any information,' said one of the officers. 'We'll be seeing you from time to time.'

After they had left I went into the cottage, sat down on the sofa and ruminated. Why, I asked myself, am I so deeply upset by the events? Was I overreacting? What would Jeannie have thought? It was easy to answer that question. She had the love for Minack that Scarlett O'Hara had for Tara. She believed that Minack, and this wild section of the Cornish coast, was a symbol of tranquillity, unsullied by tawdry opportunism, unsullied by material exploitation, unsullied by the deviousness of the human race.

I knew what Jeannie would have said . . . 'Defend it! Defend it!'

There was innocence along this Cornish cliff, the innocence of true values, an innocence which had drawn us to it those years ago, drawn us away from a way of life we had come to despise. As I said in *A Gull on the Roof*:

The glamour and the hospitality act as a narcotic, doping the finer instincts of living, and in the grey hours of early morning you lie awake painfully aware that you live in a flashy world where truth and integrity are for the most part despised, that you live in a flashy world where slickness and deceit reign supreme.

IV

I was disorientated for the rest of the day. I had no wish to return to the Confusion Room. I was myself in confusion. I proceeded to dawdle, stare into space, start to do something, stop, then start on something else. Who was this person sneaking around Minack whom I had to watch out for during the coming months?

Next morning I pulled myself together. I lay in my bed staring through the window at the donkeys, Merlin and Susie, grazing in the field of Oliver land on the other side of the shallow valley, two cups of Darjeeling tea on the table beside me . . . and I ordered myself to act. This was going to be the day I would start unravelling the Confusion Room. Nothing, no one, would stop me; and so after a breakfast of tinned sliced peaches I walked down to the Confusion Room, glanced around it and was bewildered.

How was I to secure order out of the chaos? There were files containing legions of letters, empty wine cartons now filled with miscellaneous papers, diaries, press cuttings, tapes, magazines, photographs, logbooks recording our daily tasks on the flower farm over the years; and there were suitcases with more letters, notebooks and documents. Where was I to begin?

I remembered a remark of a man who had been a salvage worker at the time when Plymouth was flattened by a bombing raid. He was asked, long afterwards, how he and his colleagues could possibly begin to clear such devastation.

'Well,' he replied, 'I picked up a brick.'

Here was the answer to my self-questioning. I moved over to Labour Warms and proceeded to pull out a drawer. The drawer was my brick. On the top of a wedge of papers was a bulging grey folder. It was the Tangye Family File, notes about the Tangye family I had collected over the years.

The first stage in clearing the Confusion Room had begun.

I took out a pamphlet my father had written about the origins of the Tangye family. It was called 'The Tannegui du Chatel family of Kersant-Tremazan, Finistere, Brittany'. And there was this note by my father: 'These notes on the adventurous early days of the Family of Tannegui are published with the object of assisting further research into its history.'

My father had been a brilliantly successful barrister before the Great War, and with an outstanding career before him. He joined up in the first weeks and was to serve as an intelligence officer at the Front until the war ended. At this stage he could have returned to the Bar, but he chose instead to become a high-ranking intelligence officer in the British Army of the Rhine. It was a mistake, a mistake that can easily occur when a man of talent is faced with alternative directions at a critical moment of his career. There was no Everest to climb in the Army. His life was a plod, whereas had he returned to the legal profession it would have scintillated. However his choice was of immeasurable benefit to myself and my two older brothers. At an impressionable age we became immersed in the musical culture of Germany, and I have always been grateful for that.

I loved my father. He was fundamentally a shy man and had a brilliant brain but, while those with brilliant brains are often devoid of emotion and dominated by logic, my father was dominated by emotion. 'Don't ever try to analyse beauty,' he said to me, 'for by so doing you will destroy its magic. Just *feel* it. *Feel* the shapes of the clouds in the sky, *feel* the sight of a butterfly, *feel* music . . .'

His choice to remain in the Army, first in Cologne then in Wiesbaden, was to lead to endless financial worries. One of the worries concerned me. I was being expensively educated at Harrow, and he had a perpetual struggle to pay the fees, maintain the normal needs of a family and keep up our home at the edge of Newquay in Cornwall, at Porth. I, in the tradition of young people of any era, took his sacrifices for granted. If I saw him working at his big desk in his study at Glendorgal, it did not enter my mind that he might be wondering as to how he was going to pay next year's fees.

My mother was a darling, so full of enthusiasm for life, so selfless in her love for her three sons. There was no rivalry in our family, though in retrospect I realized that my mother showed a special caring for me.

Perhaps this was because I was the youngest, but I think it was also because she realized I was a loner, that I did not belong to the conventional scene. My two brothers belonged to that scene, and I envied them that they could mix so easily with conventional people yet, at the same time, maintain their individuality. My eldest brother Colin, as I have already told, was captain of rugby at Haileybury, and head of his house; and he was to be the backbone of my generation of the Tangye family all his life. My brother Nigel won the King's Dirk at the Royal Naval College, Dartmouth, the equivalent of the Sandhurst Sword of Honour; and he became renowned for his futuristic design of the aircraft which featured in the H. G. Wells film *The Shape of Things to Come*.

What of Derek?

He was called into his housemaster's study the day he had dropped a catch on the boundary in a crucial inter-house cricket match and was told: 'You're useless to society Tangye!' It so happened that on the same day results had come through of an important examination. Once again I had failed it.

My father in his pamphlet tells of the two brothers, Guillaume du Chatel and Tannegui du Chatel. The former was killed during a battle with the English in 1403, and the following year Tannegui du Chatel, Chamberlain of the King, Provost of Paris and Grand Master of the King's Household, set out for England with four hundred men-at-arms to avenge his brother's death. He landed at Dartmouth and for two months roamed the coastal regions of the West Country before returning to Brittany 'laden with heavy booty', as a report of the times stated.

My father in his pamphlet developed a theory about the consequences of these two months. The first Cornish mention of a name similar to 'Tangye' in any Cornish record was that of John Taynggy in 1459, and this was followed in 1468 with William Tange. Then there came the first time when the name was spelt as it is today: the recording of the marriage in 1582 between George Tangye and Margaret Gelbart at Camborne. My father's theory was that the originator of these names was Tannegui du Chatel, during the course of his two-month raid of the West Country. Or was the originator a humble Breton from a coastal village like Camaret? It was traditional for many years to have 'onion men' calling at houses in this country, Bretons who carried their wares tied on long caterpillar-like strips. Jeannie and I had one such onion man who called once a year at Minack. He came from Camaret . . . and his name was Tangui.

There was a lull in the history of the Tangye family until the middle of the nineteenth century. None of the Tangyes seemed to have done anything of distinction. They appeared to be worthy, normal members of the Cornish community and were devoted Quakers. They centred around Camborne, Redruth and Illogan, and there was a Tangie on 1 September 1608 who was buried at Madron near Penzance. There was no clue in this background that by the middle of the nineteenth century the Tangye name was to become world famous, but this is what happened. In the file I found the manuscript I had written outlining the story of the four Tangye brothers who went to Birmingham and created a great engineering industry.

Their home was in Broad Lane, Illogan. Their father had a shop in Broad Lane, and also ten acres of land which he used to plough in Quaker dress and broad-rimmed hat. The sons, however, had no intention of following this quiet profession; and in any case they each had the qualities of genius: Richard and George were the ones with the business flair; Joseph and James, particularly James, were the inventors. So in due course these four left Illogan to find fortune in the Midlands, and, within twenty years, they had founded the Cornwall Works in Birmingham where two thousand people were to be employed, and had also made the Tangye name world famous for its engineering products.

Richard, my grandfather who died many years before I was born, was a remarkable man. His own grandfather came from St Columb near Newquay, where he worked as a boy on a farm. He was still a boy when he decided to set out for the tin mines of West Cornwall, and he walked on his own, except for his small dog, all the way to Illogan carrying on his back his only possession, a saddle. There he obtained a night job in the mines, and shortly after some rough land of rocks and gorse, and this he worked at during the day. He lived to his nineties, and Richard describes in one of his books how the old man died. A *Citizen Kane* kind of end . . . for he relived that walk from St Columb to Illogan, and his last words were: 'Has the little dog come in yet?'

Often the inventions of the brothers came before their

39

time. A bicycle proved a failure because it seemed to be so unusual; and the 'road locomotive' was a failure because the landed gentry were afraid that their horses would take flight at the sight and the sound of it. But the 'road locomotive' was a remarkable achievement. The Tangye brothers called it the Cornubia; and it could travel at twenty miles an hour and carry ten people. The first Cornubia was on the road in the early 1860s and created enormous public interest; and the brothers were right to believe they were about to make their fortune. But the landed gentry had powerful friends in Parliament; and as a consequence an act was passed forbidding any machine to proceed along the highway at more than four miles an hour, and even then it had to have a man walking in front holding a red flag. (Had but the legislators foreseen what would be happening a hundred years later!) But the Tangye brothers were not deterred. They scrapped the Cornubia, sold those in stock to Maharajahs in India, and set about developing other inventions.

They had already enjoyed one major success; this was an improved version of the hydraulic jack which on a day in January 1858 was to create a legend. Isambard Brunel had built his steamship the *Great Eastern*, and found he was unable to launch her. She was built in the Millwall Docks in London, and because of her great size she had to be launched broadside on. Everything started well, but for safety reasons the launch had to be stopped after the ship had only moved a few feet. After that, it simply wouldn't budge.

Brunel knew that he needed a lot more jacks to move the ship and he knew where to get them, hydraulic jacks which had more power than had ever been known before. The Tangye brothers still at that time had only a small workshop in Birmingham which was down an entry behind a baker's shop, and it was there that Brunel's agent one dark evening rang the bell, sure that he must have come to the wrong place. He apologized for his mistake when Richard opened the door. 'I'm looking for Tangyes,' the man explained. 'Mr Brunel needs their jacks to launch the *Great Eastern*!' For ever afterwards Richard used to say until the words became a folklore: 'We launched the *Great Eastern*, and the *Great Eastern* launched us!

Twenty years later another moment of fame came when their jacks hoisted Cleopatra's Needle into position on the Victoria Embankment within sight of the River Room at the Savoy from where Jeannie and I used often to look out upon it. Cleopatra's Needle had had an adventurous voyage from Egypt, and once here the problem had begun as to how it was to be put into place. No engineer had faced such a problem before. The year was 1878. Cleopatra's Needle had been shipped along the Thames and was anchored in its appointed position, but how to raise it? It was achieved by a Tangye jack which still lies there, along with worthy companions including a map of the London of the time, the book of Genesis in Arabic and Hebrew, copies of the newspapers of the day, weights and measures, and copies of the Bible in various languages. I have often walked along the Embankment, or looked down upon the obelisk from the Savoy windows, and felt proud that my family played a leading part in placing it there.

Richard's flair for publicity didn't let the occasion go by and the following was placed in advertisements world wide:

AD 1586 Fontana raised the Obelisk in Rome with 960 capstans, worked by 960 workmen and 75 horses.

AD 1836 Le Bas raised the Luxor Obelisk in Paris with 10 capstans worked by 480 men.

AD 1878 John Dixon raised Cleopatra's Needle using four of Tangye's Patent Hydraulic Jacks, worked by four men.

Richard, apart from his business acumen, was a man of liberal ideas. He was a great philanthropist, kept to strict rules of honour throughout his life, believed his work people were as good as himself and that they should always receive a fair reward for their work. He expected their loyalty as a result (there were never any strikes at the Cornwall Works), and that the job of a great industrialist was to be paternal. His paternalism certainly produced reforms.

He was the first industrialist in Britain to introduce the nine-hour day, the first to give a half-day on Saturday, the first to pay wages on a Friday, the first to provide a canteen for the workers, and the first to provide a free health service. These reforms were strongly supported by all the brothers, but they caused displeasure among other industrialists; for the reforms were taking place at the end of the nineteenth century, and the industrial barons resented the Tangye brothers for weakening their autocratic power by a liberal example.

Richard, in fact, could have become a politician of note. He was repeatedly asked to stand for a Birmingham constituency and he was urged to do so by Gladstone. Lord Roseberry also was anxious that he should enter politics, but the prospect of doing so did not appeal to him. Nor did he believe in honours. He refused an offer of a peerage, and only in the end accepted his knighthood because he truly believed that it was a compliment to the people of the Cornwall Works.

Unlike his brothers he had had a formal education. He was educated at the Friends' School in Sidcot, Somerset, until he was eighteen, and for the last two years he had been an apprentice teacher. It was during this period that he became fascinated by the world far beyond his confined existence. The British Empire was at its zenith and he was determined that one day he would visit all parts of it; and he did. I marvel at his energy and his boldness in carrying out his travels, sailing in small boats, unperturbed by the discomfort. He always made daily notes describing his travels, and in due course he had them privately published. He was also a great collector, and he specialized in Wedgwood pottery. He and his brother George created the finest collection of Wedgwood pottery in the world, and then presented it to the City of Birmingham. He was a great reader and historian. His Quaker upbringing turned him into being a disciple of Oliver Cromwell, and he wrote a definitive book about the period. It was called *The Two Protectors – Oliver and Richard Cromwell*.

Richard's biographer was called Stuart Reid and in the book he gives a charming description of Richard's grandfather, the one who had walked as a boy from north Cornwall to find work in the tin mines of West Cornwall accompanied by his little dog. The following passage gives a clue to Richard's own character:

The gentle, kindly old man had children who grew up to call him blessed. He was not given to many words. He was content to let his life speak instead. It spoke of faith, courage, duty, for his character was like a bit of granite with flowers growing in the crevices of the rock. He was always poor, but he contrived somehow to help other people in their time of need, for he held all that he had as a trust, and he taught his children to do the same, and to redeem whatever opportunities came to them, as life broadened out before their advancing footsteps. The words which such a man speaks to his children on the threshold of life in the magic circle of home, are not heard by the world. But, to the heart of a loyal and trustful son, no words possess more vitality. They sink deep, and like seed sown in good ground, they bear fruit.

I had no interest in my grandfather's life and those of my forebears during my adolescence. I have regretted this ever since. In my youth I became conditioned into accepting that the Tangye firm never paid a dividend and that it was always struggling for survival, providing much stress to my father who was chairman for a while and trying to save the company from extinction. The company always produced remarkable engineering projects, but they never made a profit. This situation, as I was to learn later, was the result of the third-generation syndrome, the syndrome which regularly dictates that a business once run by the men who created it often collapses when the third generation takes over.

I was, nevertheless, very conscious of the prestige of Tangyes and I was constantly reminded of this by a gimmick which made people aware of the company although they might not have any interest in its products. Tangyes had a large advertisement at the entrance to every railway station, and in the station itself, which shouted the message in blue against a white background: TANGYES' PUMPS. It was an extraordinary example of destiny that two sisters, after the day working in London, always arranged to meet by this advertisement at St Pancras Station before joining the train to take them back to St Albans. Those two girls were Jeannie and her sister Barbara.

Meanwhile I was going through the initial stages of growing up, feeling very introverted and unsure of myself, full of inhibitions, having exploratory times with girls – in love, out of love, always puzzled as to what reaction of the girl concerned might have towards me, never confident that she had any interest in me, wondering often who I really was because of the contradictions which prevailed in my character, and always, of course, worried about my future.

At an early stage I started to keep a diary, using it as a kind of confessional, reciting in the diary details of my youthful life in no rational or logical way. My confessions were a verbal outburst, like talking to a friend who I was aware would never exploit them for a gossipy purpose. I have kept a diary ever since, spasmodically because one must never be dominated by a diary. I use it now as if I have been travelling on a long journey, and I look back on the road remembering vividly things past and usually finding that the mistakes I made then I still make. All my diaries are somewhere in the Confusion Room, and I will find them. Indeed I have just found one in Labour Warms beside the Tangye File. It is my first diary, the diary of adolescence. It begins when I was at Harrow, and the time which immediately followed; and the story of first love.

June 21st.

Here it is my last term at Harrow, and I've been a failure. I have had my good moments. I was chosen captain of the junior cricket eleven of The Park, my House, and then captain of the football team. Middleditch, my stupid but amiable housemaster, said that I was the best junior captain he had ever known; and two years afterwards I saw with my own eyes in the minutes of the House 'that Benn [that year's captain] was not nearly as good as Tangye'. Naturally such early success gave me confidence for the future, and so I found it incredible that when I reached my last year I was never given any place of authority, and when two boys junior to myself were made sixth formers [prefects] I was furious then very upset. And so here I am today, a month before the end of my school career writing this diary as a nobody.

But I have come to believe there may be compensations for such failure. Perhaps I'm just trying to excuse myself, but I'm thinking that failure at school does more good to one than success. My theory is that the time at school is really only a run through for what adult life is going to be like. My failures, and these include failing at every examination that I should have passed [like my Harrovian predecessor Winston Churchill!], has made me better prepared to meet the shock and buffets of the real world which I will be facing. I will be better prepared to cope with them than a boy who has become overconfident by success, and who believes that life outside will be just as easy. I am only nineteen but I have this inner belief that struggle, and by beating struggle, is the way that a young person can become a real person. Am I just making excuses to try to boost my confidence? Only my life as it unfolds will provide the answer.

November 24th.

For five weeks I've been an office boy in Unilever working in Blackfriars House on the Embankment. I can't say I'm enjoying it! I'm at the beck and call of the clerks. 'Fetch me a cup of tea, Tangye!' But I'm learning a lot. I mean all sorts of angles are opening up for me which were closed to me when I was at Harrow. It is making me aware that there is no neat, logical development of a child's mind. I realize, for instance, that like so many others I am a late developer, and that it is ludicrous to judge a child's ability on the basis of examination results. The realization makes me happy. It is marvellous to realize that we are all individuals, not just cogs.

Yet oh dear, where am I going?

February 4th.

Have just had a fortnight's holiday in Cornwall and Glendorgal was as beautiful as ever. And while I was there I kept reading Marcel Proust, the French philosophical writer. I read again *Swann's Way*, the first part of his novel *Remembrance of Things Past*, and it is for me a sensational beginning. I find in his writings those snatches of wisdom, those answers to subconscious questions that I search for in every minute of my life. His description of a man in love describes his innermost feelings, feelings that I have had but which I've never been able to pin down or penetrate. As I read on I'm going to learn so much from his writings.

March 20th.

I've left my lodgings at Harrow, and I've now a place of my own, two rooms and a bathroom on the top floor of 38 Cranley Gardens, five minutes walk from the South Kensington Underground Station. It is marvellous. I am on my own, I am free. I'm trying to write because I am thinking of taking up journalism, and if I had the money I would take a journalism course. There is no future for me at Unilever. It just isn't the way of life I want to lead. Funny, but here I am in London, and I don't know a soul. And the only person I've got an introduction to is a family called Lubbock whose daughter is to be presented at Court this year and therefore will have lots of parties.

May 10th.

Fantastic. I was invited as a dinner guest for the first of the Lubbock girl's dances, and this has opened up all sorts of exciting occasions which leave me weary-eyed at the office. I have, in fact, become a deb's delight, deluged with invitations, and I have become quite a snob! I had a marvellous evening yesterday. The dinner party was at Claridge's in a private room, and I was the chosen partner of Florence Scheftel, the girl who was considered to be the Deb of the Year. Others at the dinner were those whom I regularly see in the fashionable magazines, people like Alan Pryce Jones, Katherine Horlick, Baba Beaton, Hamish St Clair Erskine

who wore a flowing cloak . . . and then we went on to Liza
Maugham's dance in the King's Road where her mother
Syrie Maugham lives. It was all so elegant. I danced with
Liza [Somerset Maugham's daughter], an ethereal, wistful
girl, the beautiful Dot Hyson, Unity Mitford, Bee Lillie, and
so on. Tomorrow night is the Bowes Lyon dance, and the
following night the Duchess of Norfolk's dance at Norfolk
House in St James's Square. All such fun, but oh so exhausting, and it makes facing the office drearier and drearier.

June 16th.

My very first writing success. I sent an article called
'Archers Invade England' to the *News Chronicle*, and today I
received a letter saying 'they hoped to make use of it quite
soon'. I can't believe it. My writing career has begun!

June 20th.

It is all happening . . . I went on my own to see a revue at
the Comedy Theatre called *Ballyhoo*. I sat there up in the
Upper Circle, and looked down on the stage and saw a girl
whom I thought was the most beautiful I had ever seen. She
was dark and slim and wearing very little, and dancing with
a man to a song called 'Mediterranean Madness', a haunting
melody which ever since has lingered in my mind. I was
captivated. Next evening I went back to the Comedy
Theatre, and again the next evening. I had become obsessed
by the girl.

June 21st.

Of all the things that could have happened . . . today on
my way to the office in the Underground I was reading the

Daily Express, and suddenly I saw *her* on the Show Page, and there was the caption, 'Pearl Argyle, the prettiest ballet dancer in London'. So that is her name. And the paragraph went on to say that she was twenty, born in South Africa, and had come to London to train with the Ballet Rambert Company, and that she had made a sensational success and that film companies were clamouring for her. What can I do? I'm crazy for her, but how can I compete with all the sophisticated famous men who must be after her? Me a clerk, a lowly clerk at that, in Unilever?

June 22nd.

At three o'clock this morning as I lay awake I had an idea. I was tossing and turning, dominated by this mad love for such an unobtainable girl when I had this idea. Her suitors, I said to myself, would always be lavish with their attentions. So why don't I try the opposite? I've got nothing to lose. Thus I went today to a florist and asked that only six red roses should be delivered to Miss Pearl Argyle at the Comedy Theatre, accompanied by my note which read:

> Dear Pearl Argyle, I *so* admire you. I am twenty one years old and I have no special qualifications. But I have been three times in a week watching your performance in *Ballyhoo*, and I cannot tell you how I *long* to meet you. Would it be possible for you to have a drink and early supper with me at the Berkeley before the theatre next Tuesday? I give you my address but I don't expect you to answer. In order to recognize me, should you think it possible to come (which I don't expect), I will have a red carnation in my buttonhole.

June 26th.

I'm in such a high state of tension. It is seven-thirty in the morning, and I'm just writing these notes because I want to put down my worst fears, my expected fears that I will be standing there in the Berkeley, carnation in my button-hole, and there is no sign of her. And after all why should there be any sign of her? I've got absolutely nothing to offer her. I am a clerk. She knows nothing about me. I have no meaning for her. What madness that I should even hope she might respond.

June 27th.

But she did.

June 28th.

I will look back on the moment all my life as one of the most exciting, unexplainable. I was standing by a pillar in the small foyer of the Berkeley that faces on Piccadilly, minutes ticking away, no sign of her, the youth of smart London which use the Berkeley as their personal club greeting each other in extravagant language as they passed by me . . . me watching the entrance.

And there she was.

In black velvet. Dark hair over her shoulders, high cheek-bones in a small face, small, a slender body, utterly bewitch-ing. I went up to her. 'I'm Derek,' I said. She looked at me bemused, bewildered, then said shyly, nervously: 'I can't think why I am here!' I too was bewildered. I couldn't think of anything to say in reply.

But I had an ally. I had confided as soon as I arrived at the Berkeley my coming predicament to Ferraro who, as everyone knows, is the famous restaurant manager who nurtures the love affairs of the young at the Berkeley by paying special attention to a couple, thus giving them confidence . . . and this is how he acted with Pearl and me. There I was stuttering an introduction when he suddenly appeared at my elbow. 'How nice to see you, Mr Tangye, I have a table reserved for you.' And he guided us to a discreet table beside a curtained window.

I was not happy. Here I had my dream girl with me, but I felt clumsy and I was aware of the shadow of all those romantic suitors, older and wiser, and so much more experienced as to how to entertain such a creature. I was made dumb by the thought of them, and I gushed out remarks as they came into my head, remarks which seemed to have no effect on her. She looked beautiful, so beautiful that I just wanted to look at her, saying nothing. And when the supper was over and she had left to go to the Comedy Theatre, I was sure the occasion had been a complete failure and I would never see her again.

June 30th.

I've had a letter from her. I couldn't believe it. A letter thanking me, and saying she had enjoyed herself very much.

July 2nd.

She rang me up at 38 Cranley Gardens. I wasn't there but she left a message asking me to have drinks with her at her flat in Hanover Square on Sunday, then go on to the Ballet Rambert at Notting Hill Gate. I couldn't believe it. It sounds as if she likes me.

July 5th.

It's past midnight but I just must tell what a wonderful time I have had. Her flat is in the top of a block in Hanover Square, and no one else was there. It was no longer the numb mood of the Berkeley. She was animated. We had lots to say. There seemed to be so much in common. It was effortless. Not in my wildest dreams did I ever expect to be so at ease with her. We loved the same music, the same pictures, the same attitude towards people. And then we went on to the Ballet Club and in the interval she introduced me to Freddie Ashton, Diana Gould and to Madame Rambert herself. I admit I felt a bit self-conscious. I felt they were looking at me, and saying to themselves: 'Pearl has found a new one. What does she find in him?'

July 10th.

She is so utterly unspoilt, I cannot define my feeling for her. She inspires me. I've actually been writing and I feel she is driving me to be a writer, she has so much in common with me. Yesterday evening we went to see a film at the Plaza, she being free in the evenings at last because *Ballyhoo* had to come off, and afterwards I asked her where she would like to go for supper. She said she didn't care whether we went to a Lyons or an ABC . . . but I ignored this and took her to the Berkeley. And while we were there she said how she longed to see *Tosca* at Covent Garden, that it would be one of the most exciting moments of her life if she could do so. *Tosca* was being sung at Covent Garden the following week . . . And I made a mental note that I *had* to borrow the money for two top-price tickets, then take her to supper afterwards.

July 15th.

Oh, so wonderful! *Tosca* went off with a divine swing, ideal seats in the stalls, distinguished people all around us, and I having an ego trip of seeing people nudging each other and looking our way at Pearl. And then at the end when Edith Turner was taking her bow to a continuous roll of applause, Pearl was on her feet calling out, 'Bravo! Bravo!' It was an unforgettable experience for me who has loved Puccini ever since I was a child going to the Opera House in Cologne.

I had already decided there was only one place to take her afterwards, and that was the Savoy Grill. I had never been there, but I guessed that if I booked a table saying Pearl Argyle would be a guest they would take me seriously although they did not know my name. And it is exactly what happened.

We were given the table close to the Strand Entrance to the Grill through the small foyer, a table which is reserved for those who are wanting to be noticed, or who others in the restaurant would like to notice. Thus it was with Pearl. She had no sooner sat down when Lady Oxford and Asquith appeared at our table, and charmingly said how she had loved Pearl's dancing in *Ballyhoo*. And then other people came to our table, all congratulating Pearl while I sat totally silent, wanting to hide myself. Mary Ellis was one, and George Robey, who made us burst into laughter by his imitation of Chaliapin. I am sure I will never forget such an evening.

July 29th.

I'm not happy. I thought it was such a wonderful evening that she would have written me a wonderful letter. It was a nice letter, but that's all. Then this evening I had a nasty shock. I met Billy Walker, who produced *Ballyhoo*, by chance in the King's Road, and he said that Pearl had gone to Paris for a few days with an American from Hollywood. I felt so upset, so jealous, so betrayed in fact.

August 5th.

I heard she was back, and I did such a silly thing. All the result of the jealousy feeling. I took a bus to Hanover Square at around midnight, and hung around there, watching for a light in her flat, watching for anyone arriving, and I saw no one. And I had to walk all the way back to Cranley Gardens because no bus was then running.

August 10th.

All well, so to speak. A sweet letter this morning which gave me comfort but not satisfaction. I must give her up. There is no future with her. There is no permanent relationship to aim for because we are much too young, and our careers are just beginning. Yes, the story is ended.

September 30th.

I haven't contacted her. It doesn't help. I'm in love with her. I must realize this. But if we are not in contact I guess my love will dim.

October 10th.

A letter from her, and my heart dances. She has moved from Hanover Square to a mews flat near Claridge's and she writes asking me to see it and suggests going to the Russian Ballet at the Alhambra Leicester Square afterwards. And of course I forget all my denying intentions and accept, and how wonderful that I did. She took me round afterwards to meet the stars who had conquered London – Massine, Danilova, Baronova . . . and I found that these Russian stars were treating Pearl as one of them. Poor Pearl. She, I know is going through that torment of change . . . should I remain a dancer or become a film star? But Hollywood is chasing her. 'Derek,' she said to me that evening, 'all my feelings are that I should be a dancer.' And then as if she was pleased that I believed in her talent as a dancer, 'You do feel that, don't you?'

We are now on a level of special companionship again. Effortless. She rings me up, and we talk about little things. We meet, go to a film, have supper together in my two rooms in Cranley Gardens, talk about our future, wonderfully young, all the years ahead of us to make mistakes.

October 20th.

I am so inexperienced. I don't know how to handle such a situation. I feel a young man or girl should first meet someone who can lead them through all the mysteries of a love affair, all the opposites which attack you, explain all the contrary emotions, the hopes, the fears, the stupid misunderstandings . . .

October 25th.

I might say that the impossible has happened. It would be both conceited and wrong if I do so. After all why should she have a special affection for me when there are so many brilliant men pursuing her? There is nothing tangible about me that can appeal to her. I just want to love her. Yet she rang me just now and has asked me to go with her to a film party given by John Sutro the day after next. Of course I accepted, trying to hide my delight.

November 1st.

It was a conventional party where everyone shouted and nobody heard what was being said, and anyhow were looking over the shoulders of those whom they were talking to, wondering how they could escape from their present companion. But in my case I did not have to trouble. No one took the slightest notice of me. All eyes were on exquisite Pearl. And then the party neared its end, and we left together, and it was such a strange, yet unfulfilled feeling that I was leaving with the girl who was the star of the evening. She was looking so beautiful, so naturally beautiful, and we went from the party to the Café Royal. We had a table on the balcony looking down on the floor below; and there now began a scene which was so delightful. We both rippled away, conversing without any effort. Then she said something that so surprised me, so touched me. 'Oh, Derek,' she said, 'I have been so looking forward to this evening all the week!' Then she went on: 'So often you look forward to an evening, and it doesn't mean you enjoy it . . . but oh Derek I'm enjoying this one!' Then she added: 'I really worried that you might telephone me and put me off!'

We left the Café Royal at midnight. It was a calm evening and she said she would like to walk, not taking the taxi I suggested.

We crossed Regent Street, then along Burlington Street, past Burlington Arcade and into Bond Street. We were holding hands. We made spasmodic remarks, but there was no conversation. A strange silence was binding us. We were utterly content just being together, no forced hassle, a period of time when life appeared to be effortless. We walked up Bond Street, passing the prostitutes who were waiting in doorways, past Sotheby's, past the long-established shops that have made Bond Street the most romantic shopping street in the world . . . and then we turned off at Bruton Street and a few yards later turned right to the narrow Avery Row which led to Pearl's mews flat with its windows stretching up Bruton Mews.

'And now the evening is ended,' I said.

'Why?' she asked.

Pearl married a German refugee film director a couple of years later; and she died in Hollywood when still in her twenties.

V

I was in touch with the CID from time to time though nothing significant occurred. 'Wait till April' they warned me.

Meanwhile I was having a pleasant, productive early spring; and the spring at Minack begins in late January and early February, the time when the first daffodils are ready to bloom. I had the quiet pleasure of walking round the daffodil meadows, and the satisfaction of beginning the next stage of the Confusion Room investigation. This stage, I had decided, involved the metal filing cabinet containing a multitude of correspondence . . . including two special files, the J.T. and the D.T. files.

It was always a hazardous business, in the days Jeannic and I were selling daffodils for market, to estimate when they would be ready. A cold spell in January, delaying them, would make us become anxious that they would coincide with up-country daffodils, thus spoiling our prices. Then suddenly the temperature would rise and within twenty-four hours there would be a deluge of daffodils to pick, and they would almost swamp us.

This year, when the CID were keeping a watch, this year when, for the first time, the deceit of someone in our modern society had invaded our daffodil world, it was climatically normal. The various kinds of daffodils bloomed in a normal progression, and as I wandered round the meadows it was such a pleasure for me not to worry, just to be able to look and to marvel that they were no longer commercial entities; no longer were they to be gathered from their beautiful surroundings, no longer going on a long journey which would lead them to an eventual dustbin. They would dance through the spring, fields of them, shining their freedom to all who came to see them.

I first went up the two steps leading from the patio known as the bridge into the Lama field. It was across this field and down the two steps that Jane of *A Drake at the Door* used to come from the cottage where she lived with her mother in primitive happiness without electric light and with the water coming from a well. She was only fourteen when she first worked for us, trimming tomato plants in the greenhouses. She had a brother, Jeremy, who one day arrived at our door carrying a dark blue velvet cushion on which had been stitched in gold letters the name 'Monty'. Monty was the cat Jeannie and I had brought from London with us and was the hero of *A Cat in the Window*; the cushion, stitched by Jane's mother, was a tribute to him. He had just died.

The field was called the Lama field because Lama, the little black cat who adopted us after Monty, used to treat it as her special terrain. It was here we had planted the deep yellow daffodil called Joseph

McLeod, so named after a famous BBC news announcer during the Hitler war by a Dutchman in Rotterdam who bred it. One night his house was raided by German soldiers searching for secret radios. The Dutchman hid his radio in time, and after the soldiers had gone he switched it on and heard the announcer end the news bulletin with the words: 'And this was Joseph McLeod reading it.' The Dutchman looked at the little seedling which was standing in a pot on the mantelpiece and had a brilliant idea. He would celebrate his escape that evening by calling the seedling Joseph McLeod.

I stood there for a while staring at the field, as I had done year after year since we first excitedly planted the bulbs. It was like greeting old friends who had reappeared after a long interval. It was always thus in January and early February at Minack. Jeannie and I used to feel reassured when we saw the green shoots and buds in the meadows and the hedges. The rhythm of life had not changed, and our minds were free of media turmoil and passing fashions. We could ignore the smug hypocrisy which chases people in public life. We could be aware that truth is indestructible. Truth is simplicity. It can be understood in a few words. It does not require long explanations from theorists.

I left the Joseph McLeod field, sad that there were increasing patches where the bulbs had died out so there were barren areas resembling an attack of mange, and proceeded across what we once called the donkey field, where Penny and Fred used to roam, to the wood. Here I knew there would be secret daffodils growing, here and there, out in odd corners; and when I found one it was my habit to behave in the same way as the Prince of Wales was ridiculed for doing. He was described, if you remember, as the loony Prince for admitting he talked to the flowers in his garden. Such a display of derision heightens the superficiality of the media. For financial reasons, the media are not interested in the everyday emotions of sensitive people. Only the effect of a story is considered, the surface effect. Circulation is paramount. Sincerity is expendable.

But I am loony. Here I was talking to a daffodil which had reappeared after a year's absence and which, because of the vagaries of nature, had not bloomed the year before. The sight prompted me to reminisce to myself, remembering incidents which were precious to me, and secret. I was part of that very personal world into which no one can intrude. The conversation with one's original being, before one was pushed to conform. Utter naturalness. Freedom from convention.

I strolled back to the cottage and then down to the cliff meadows that border the coastal path. On the left was a meadow containing California, and on the right was a meadow of miniature daffodils called Obvallaris. Such an ugly name for such a pretty daffodil. We once sent a consignment of them to Carlo Naeff, head of the famous Covent Garden sales group J. and E. Page, together with some from other meadows . . . and the

Harrods buyer saw them and bought them all for a display in Harrods' entrance hall.

In other years I would not have turned back, but would have walked down to the early cliff meadows. These were the meadows which fell like a vineyard down to the rocks and the sea, and were where we always picked Magnificence, the earliest of the daffodils to be ready for market on a Cornish cliff. After we had bunched them, and Jeannie had packed them, twenty-four bunches in a sales box, I would take them in the Land-Rover to Penzance Station to be greeted by porters on the flower train platform, porters like George Mills and Donald with their welcome shout: 'You're the first!' Yes, Minack cliff grew very early daffodils, daffodils which had romance in their petals for they were natural, living on the cliffs beside the sea . . . not forced daffodils in greenhouses far away from the sea, forced daffodils which eliminated the magic of spring.

But this time I did not make my way to the cliff meadows. 'Damn, blast,' I murmured to myself. 'Damn, blast the bastard who has vandalized our cliff.'

I returned to the cottage, then went up the lane across Monty's Leap and on to the solitude gate where stands the sign 'A PLACE FOR SOLITUDE' in memory of Jeannie, which I had taken to her just before she died; and which she kissed, not knowing that she was dying.

I climbed into the field, celandines spattering the grass, two magpies coarsely cackling around the ground where Merlin and Susie were munching. They looked up and came towards me, and soon they were

nudging me, expecting I had brought them biscuits –
which I hadn't. On my left was Jeannie's Shelter, and
suddenly I had an intense desire for her, a nostalgic
gush, and I remembered again what the Queen Mother
said when someone asked her how she managed to
appear cheerful after King George VI died. 'You
should see me in my private moments,' she replied.

I had put much thought into creating Jeannie's Shelter and, in Pisces fashion, had changed my mind again
and again as to where it should be erected. The object
was to have half of it providing a home for the Leyland
tractor and a store for hay and straw; and the other half
as a home for the donkeys. More accurately, a second
home which would be convenient for me. No longer
would I have to lead them, when the weather was very
rough, to the stables beside the cottage. They would be
free to do what they liked. They could, if they so liked,
return to the Minack stables by the track they had
created in the shallow valley, a very marshy track in
winter. The cost of the shelter came from the money
that Jeannie had left, and so it was her very own, her
personal memorial to her life at Minack. There is a
sentimental bonus to this story. The shelter was
erected by a father and son called Hepworth, and from
the moment I first met them I knew they would have
become friends of Jeannie. They were in sympathy,
they understood my emotional fears, and by their dedica-
tion to their work they calmed me and made me happy
that such a couple were the creators of her shelter.

I left the donkeys in sulky mood and walked across

the field along what is known as the M walk to the honeysuckle meadow where Ambrose lies and Oliver, and the memories of Jeannie. Ascania violets were in bloom beneath a hedge, three Sol d'Or shone their deep yellow in front of the little bench with Obvallariva emerging around them. On the bank behind the bench there were snowdrops and more violets. I stood there staring across the moorland towards the rocky promontory of Carn Barges, the sea of Mount's Bay behind; and I thought of that moment when we had stood there and saw Minack for the first time, and knew that we were looking at our destiny.

In the introduction to *The World of Minack*, which I dedicated '*To Jeannie's dream*,' I wrote:

Jeannie had a passion for Minack like that of Scarlett O'Hara of *Gone with the Wind*, for Tara. Minack was an obsession. She believed it belonged to those needing solitude and time for contemplation, to the birds, to the insects, the grass, the wild flowers, the animals, the bracken, the rocks, and to those of any age who yearn to be free of the conventional environment in which they are trapped . . . and she had this dream that we might find a way to keep Minack undisturbed for posterity, not just for those who might come here, but for the imagination of those who will never be able to come here.

Then I added:

There has been a beginning. Minack Cottage, which is rented from the estate of an old and distinguished Cornish family, has been Listed Grade II by the Department of the

Environment because of the Minack Chronicles; and because of its seventeenth-century antiquity. So it is now a part of the English Heritage.

The Minack Chronicles Trust, meanwhile has been formed to take care of the twenty acres . . . which, as I tell in *The Ambrose Rock*, we were lucky to buy. There are four Trustees, and there are Associate Trustees, several of whom live overseas. They feel, each of them, that Minack has meant something special to them, and that they will do everything they can to preserve it . . . But they will have to be on guard, as I am on guard. There will always be those who are ready to pounce on tranquillity. There will always be those intent on mutilating nature. There will always be those who are blind to beauty.

The solitude seekers are a different breed from those who prefer to march the countryside in groups. Such groups choose such a way of embracing the countryside because of the company, the chatter, the pleasure of being organized. The solitude seekers, on the other hand, hate being organized, hate to chatter. They are sensitive people who find an inward strength by being alone, by being silent amongst nature; and it is such people who belong to Minack. One of the rewards that has come from the Minack Chronicles is that I can say to someone, a reader, who may call: 'Go and wander. Forget about time, relax. No groups will interrupt your solitude.' Heaven knows one cannot guarantee the future, but one can do one's best.

The cottage, as I have said, is English-Heritage listed because of the Minack Chronicles. The Charity

Commissioners have designated our trust, the Derek and Jeannie Tangye Minack Chronicles Trust, to be a literary trust which has been given certain objectives to fulfil, but they have safeguards. The conditions surrounding these objectives, are included in my will:

The object of the Charity is to advance the education of the public about the Minack Chronicles and any other literary work, and that of the literary work and illustration work of Jean Tangye published under her maiden name of Jean Nicol and *in particular by preserving Oliver land as a place of solitude* to which the public may have access *under the supervision* of my Trustees the better to understand the Minack Chronicles and my other literary work.

I left the honeysuckle meadow and went up the undergrowth-bordered path to the Ambrose Rock, and heaved myself up on it. It is a pleasant place to contemplate, and I was in the mood to contemplate Jeannie. I had a sense of comfort that she was pleased with what I was trying to do to fulfil her dream, and I found myself also contemplating as to why our marriage had been such a happy one. It was, I believe, because, from an orthodox point of view, we lived dangerously.

Jeannie was deliciously pretty, and she seemed never to lose the looks of youth. Ask anyone who saw her and they will tell you that. In her job of Public Relations Officer of the Savoy Hotel Group she had been constantly surrounded by the glamorous men of the time. It was a situation I accepted from the moment we began living together, and then married.

Here is an impression of Jeannie written by an American lady living in Colorado after she had read *Jeannie*:

She had such exquisite physical beauty. Your wedding photo is one of the loveliest I have ever seen. Jeannie possessed the same exquisite beauty of Vivien Leigh whom, I believe, still sets the standard of beauty across generations. Jeannie's beauty, however, has far more than a fleeting, superficial beauty. I believe she possessed a special beauty of spirit and soul, and it goes without saying that her love for creatures great and small, deeply reaches a chord within my soul.

We lived dangerously in the sense that we believed the secret of a prolonged, happy marriage is to live subtly free. I remember saying to Jeannie that I was not going to display tantrums if she wished to go out with a man, and I remember her reply which made me laugh. We had been married a week. She used a cricket phrase. 'Oh, she said, 'I like that. I like the thought that I can have a change of bowling!'

Jeannie and I never found that casual friendships caused harm, but we both realized we were lucky. We shared a base, and we were always to share one. I likened it to a harbour: we were free to sail out of the harbour, knowing that the security of it awaited our return.

A casual friendship can help in so many ways. In a marriage it can help to relieve the tensions of a couple who are growing tired of the monotony of living together. One of them meets someone who is momentarily in tune, provides excitement and enhances the day by the prospect of a meeting. Such meetings can take the pressure off a dying marriage, and revive it. In work, a casual friendship can have a similar effect. Before it became illegal, flirting, for instance, could provide fun in the office. Those concerned felt better for it.

The kill-joys, however, will not have any of this. They live in their smug cells, ignorant of the contradictory emotions of sensitive people; and so they clamour for behaviour of rigid orthodoxy. Thus, in their view, anyone in the public eye must be condemned and exposed if they have a casual friendship. Nor do they understand that throughout history the minds of creative people have been suddenly lit up by a casual friendship, and the fire of that friendship has inspired a masterpiece or a great achievement.

I returned to the cottage by way of the badger-sett country, the path with a badger home entrance in its way, along blackthorn alley, left into the Oliver land field and down towards Jeannie's Shelter. The donkeys were near by, always hopeful. I passed them with a promise that I would return with the rich tea biscuits they craved, but they would have to wait for I had other things to do. I intended to delve into the J.T. and D.T. files, and this is what I proceeded to do. I first went through them in the Confusion Room, then took away those I found interesting to the cottage where I read them again, remembering. As I sat there on the sofa, the items spread around me, I had the customary cat experience of discomfort as Cherry jumped up on the sofa and spread herself on the items I was wanting to read. Here are some of those items I liked and Cherry sat on.

A. P. Herbert, wit, once Independent Member of Parliament for Oxford University, changer of the divorce laws at that time, loved by everyone who knew him, author of musicals like *Bless the Bride* with its lovely music by Vivian Ellis, sends a note:

I was at a gathering last night with Charlie Chaplin and Danny Kaye. Somehow it came up as to why Charlie was at the Savoy while Danny, who always used to stay at the Savoy, was staying at the Dorchester, and Danny replied: 'What is the point of staying at the Savoy without Jean Nicol?'

In the scrawly handwriting of Gertrude Lawrence . . .

Hello Darlings, this is no April Fool's Day to me . . . we have got the *most terrific hit.*

Nothing has ever been produced on Broadway by anyone else that has in any way touched the public and the critics as has *The King and I.* I am sending you all the notices, and though we have only been three days, I am longing to get the play to London . . . but we shall have to wait at least three years.

I think of you both even in my busiest and most nerve-wracking days, and during the rehearsals and the road try-out, and I have often envied your peaceful meadows. I shall be sending some more packages of surprises now that all is calm again. You will go wild about *The King and I.* It is simply beautiful, touching, and most engaging and enchanting in every way, and I have had notices for my *singing*! Have been studying for four years since *Lady in the Dark*.

My love always . . . Gee.

From Gertrude Lawrence (typed):

Derek will be getting a proposition from me via the Holtzmann office which I hope he will find of interest. He could do all the early part of the book amongst all the people in England and then a flying trip here would give access to all my Pressbooks and American contacts. I want the book done by an Englishman and published at Home first. I also want the book to have frankness, wit, and warmth, and be a true accounting and to contain many things which I personally could not include when writing my Autobiography. However, as all my family are 'departed', my book *A Star Danced* will be of some help in the forming of the earlier history. All this, and because I loved his *Time was Mine*, and he is an old friend, and can get access to all the right people makes me feel that Derek should have first refusal of this job which has been in consideration here by many sources for some time. Am anxiously awaiting his reply . . . ever fondly, Gee.

From Fanny Holtzmann, Gertrude's lawyer (I had turned down the offer, saying Jeannie and I were content in the life we had chosen):

Your letters to Gertrude and me gave us much pause for thought. In fact it affected Gee so much that she was ready to follow in your footsteps. You are both to be congratulated on the courage of your convictions. How I envy you!

Nearly two years after the opening triumph of *The*

King and I came this telegram from Richard Aldrich, Gertrude's husband. 'Our Gertrude joined the immortals today.'

Some years later, a letter from Noël Coward in his neat handwriting.

My dear Derek, I was entirely enchanted by *A Donkey in the Meadow* and thanks so very much for sending it to me. Your writing is so vivid and gay and so lucid and I enjoyed every minute of it. I love Fred and I love Lama, and in fact I loved the lot . . . love Noël.

My mother was ill, and every day either Jeannie or myself wrote a letter to her. This one was written when A. P. Herbert was staying with us and Radie Harris, a famous American columnist, was due.

Today it is cold, grey, and a drizzle. Last night was spent in discussion as to what musical Alan could write next. Jeannie over breakfast had suggested *The Water Gypsies*, and apparently Vivian Ellis had also suggested this. And this morning Alan has gone down to the cabin at the bottom of our cliff meadows to start!

A very close friend of Gertrude Lawrence called Radie Harris, and who writes a very influential Broadway column, and also writes film scripts, telegraphed us yesterday asking whether she could come here for the weekend. At the moment she is working with John Huston and Gregory Peck on *Moby Dick* in Ireland. And being an inexhaustible American she proposes to take the boat from Waterford to Fishguard, and thence come on here by train. She arrives on Friday and returns on Tuesday. This means that Alan will have to give up his bed in the spare room for a campbed in the flower packing house. He is amusingly cooperative!

Now I must get back to my ploughing. I was halfway across a field yesterday when it broke down, and I had to get a part mended.

The next letter to my mother:

We are in a high state of dither because Alan pointed out that American women always travel with enormous cabin trunks, worse still, as yet (9 a.m.) we haven't heard what time Radie is arriving; and a horrifying picture has been conjured up of her arriving at Penzance, and asking a taxi driver to take her to Minack! What will she do when she finds herself, plus cabin trunk, dumped at the top by the farm? However all this is fanciful, and no doubt there will be a solution.

We are quite exhausted. A telegram yesterday morning said she was getting a later train from Cardiff. Mr Berryman who brought the telegram from Lamorna Post Office said he thought the train would get in about six. But at six when we got to the station we found it was due about seven, and then at seven we were told it was over an hour late. When finally she arrived, she said she would like to have a quick snack somewhere as there had been no dining car and she hadn't eaten since breakfast. 'Just a little smoked salmon,' she said. Of course there was no such thing in Cornwall, but we hustled her into a pub and gave her a Cornish pasty. Then we drove home, but we had forgotten she was lame and, as you know, we can only reach the cottage by driving across two fields and climbing over two hedges. It was a hazardous journey, but all was well and Radie said it was the most romantic arrival possible to a lonely, ancient Cornish cottage. And more complications. The farmer has chosen to put his cows in the field by the spare room, and there is at this very moment one cow poised just outside the window where she is sleeping. Well, the drama will unfold, and up-to-date details will be on your breakfast table tomorrow.

We had lunch yesterday while Radie had breakfast. For 365 days in the year she never goes to bed before two a.m. and never gets up before 12 noon. Alan however is whistling at us by 8 a.m., goes into the kitchen which he calls a galley, and starts washing up.

Radie has brought some of her Broadway columns to read, and they are full of showbusiness gossip. And she has such funny bitchy stories to tell us. She was at a party the other day given by Ty Power and his wife Linda Christian. Said Ty to Radie: 'Have you seen the earrings I've given Linda?' Radie goes over to Linda and admires the fabulous diamonds. 'How exquisite, Linda, dear.' Replies Linda: 'Thanks, Radie darling but' (a faint sneer in her voice) 'they are not as good as usual.' And then she told this story of Paulette Goddard. Radie was lunching with her, and admired a miraculous diamond bracelet Paulette was wearing. Says Radie: 'You and Sonja Henjie, Paulette darling, wear the most beautiful jewellery in Hollywood.' Paulette looked at her sweetly. 'But Radie darling, there is a difference. Sonja *buys* hers.'

Chaos was caused in the Lamorna pub yesterday evening as Radie rippled away about the stars, and Alan about Churchill. The fellow visitors looked solidly at their beers, pretending not to listen but listening all the time. Then Radie leant

74

across to me and said: 'I have to get hold of Gregory Peck, could you get this number for me?' That caused, as you can imagine, great interest. I went away and rang and he answered. I went back to the bar and said: 'Radie dear, Gregory Peck is on the phone.' My dear I thought everyone in the bar was going to swoon!

She told us a sad story about Gertrude. Apparently for some months before she died her voice was going, and Rodgers and Hammerstein were trying to get her out of *The King and I*. That meant they would not have had her playing at Drury Lane in any case, and that of course would have broken her heart. Radie leaves tomorrow, and it has been a hilarious time, every minute of it. Alas, Radie has yet to see the sea. We have been in a cocoon of fog the whole time.

Another letter:

We had such a happy time listening to the Proms yesterday evening. We were listening to the final movement of the Cesar Franck D-Minor symphony conducted by Malcolm Sergeant when Hubert, in the dying light, arrived on the roof and started squawling. Alan went to the door and looked up to the roof: 'Shush, Hubert,' said Alan putting a finger to his lips, 'or I'll tell Sir Malcolm!' And Hubert went silent, and remained silent. He is a remarkable gull and seems very attached to us. Yesterday afternoon I was watching Monty in the garden when Hubert began to make his demanding cries. Monty's reaction is always the same . . . he looks up at him, and then opens his mouth in a soundless snarl.

A.P.H. goes off tomorrow, and never before have we had a visitor who has stayed such a long time, and during it he has written the full script of *The Water Gypsies*, and he is going to visit Vivian Ellis who will be writing the music. Such a touching thing . . . he is very nervous. 'Will Vivian like it?' he asks nervously.

He has been so stimulating, and we have gained so much from his visit. He removed from us the everlasting round of talk about the crops, and he gave our minds a real holiday. It meant something else too. I want to write a book about Minack, and he has given me a literary atmosphere, and so I feel I may be able to get down to it, though it will take a long time to do. It is the whole fullness of his personality which is so delightful, and his utter naturalness. Then there is the gusto, the wit, and the gentleness. Yesterday he insisted on going down to the rocks, despite a cold wind, in order to collect limpets for Monty and Hubert, and you should have seen his zest and pleasure as he watched them eat them. His secret is that nothing and no one is too small or too insignificant for him to extract pleasure from. Not only does he entertain but also manages to lure the very best from his companion. He listens to a story, and never waits impatiently to jump in with one of his own. He will make his own bed, and gets a thrill out of using the Hoover, and he is always washing up . . . not in the spectacular fashion of a guest who is trying to please but just because the washing up has to be done. At this very moment he is going round the sitting room with a duster, and he is singing the song from *Bless the Bride* which he wrote with Vivian Ellis, that lovely song:

'This is my lovely day.'

VI

I finished reading the two files and returned them to the Confusion Room. What should I look for now? I saw in a corner, wedged between empty wine boxes and the end wall, a dark brown leather suitcase known by the trade name of Revelation. The Revelation suitcase was once fashionable besides being practical. Its advantage over other suitcases was that it had a device which made it expand when more was put into it. This particular suitcase in the corner of the Confusion Room was an old friend which I had not taken notice of for several years.

It had travelled the world with me. It had sailed in the Cunard liner *Aquitania* to New York, stayed at the legendary Algonquin Hotel, was with me in a Greyhound bus across America to San Francisco, been with me in Hollywood, then in Panama, then by steerage to Tahiti and other South Sea islands, then to New Zealand, Australia, Hong Kong, Shanghai, Tokyo, and back to Europe by the Trans-Siberian railway. It had also been the central feature in a curious incident involving me and the Bishop of Panama.

It was a bizarre affair. I was sailing in a Norwegian freighter which also carried up to a dozen passengers from San Pedro in California to Balboa at the entrance to the Panama Canal. The bishop and his personal priest, a young man reminding me of a weasel, used to lure me of an evening to play poker. I am not a card-playing person, but I agreed and the small amounts we gambled on mounted up. So too did the incidentals which living aboard inevitably entail. The night before arrival at Balboa came, and the settling up of debts was put into action. I had forty-five dollars which I had kept in my suitcase intact because I had no need to use cash during the voyage. The forty-five dollars comprised my wordly possessions except for a few dollars in change which had to maintain me until I set out on my voyage to Tahiti.

I went to my suitcase, the one which was before me now in the Confusion Room, and found no sign of the money. All hell was let loose when I disclosed my horror. My fellow passengers looked at me so suspiciously that the Norwegian captain summed up their views by saying: 'You never had any money. You've invented this story of the forty-five dollars. They never existed!'

Of course they did. I had kept them in the unlocked suitcase, never believing anyone would steal them. But who did steal them?

Two months later in Tahiti when I was staying in a pension on the harbour front at Papeete owned by a charming unfrocked Roman Catholic priest, I returned to my room one afternoon and opened the suitcase to bring out a shirt . . . and there neatly folded on top of the shirt were forty-five dollars! Has anyone any suggestions how they got there? I had used the suitcase daily ever since they had been missing. Could there have been any contact between the entourage of the bishop and the unfrocked priest? I had found them on the very day that the monthly steamer from Panama had arrived at Papeete.

I was now about to open the suitcase when I saw on the back of a shelf in Labour Warms the diary of my travels around the world. I was distracted by the sight of it, and I decided to have a look at it. I turned to the first few pages and I was hooked. The distant past became the present and I was once again in the Cunard liner *Aquitania*, and once again living the experience of New York. I was fascinated by seeing my handwriting describing two incidents which gave me much pleasure and excitement at the time, but which, years later, were to provide me with shocks.

The first incident, or story, began on my first night on the *Aquitania*. Here is how my diary described it.

June 27th.

No one could have a duller first crossing of the Atlantic than I. Only ninety-six cabin passengers compared with the usual three fifty. Not a pretty girl among them, all are dull, ordinary-looking individuals you'd find any day of the year in a seaside health resort. All except one.

He is Tim Mayfield, a rich young Canadian, a friend of [my] brother Nigel, and who, incredibly, had invited Nigel to go on this trip as his guest. He feels about the people as I do, and we have spent most of the time together.

He has a round, good-looking face with dark brown eyes

that always seem to be smiling. His mouth is small with a thick lower lip. He is thirty-two years old and his black hair is already thinning. He frequently strokes it with his hand as if he was conscious of it, and it was hurting his vanity.

You would think of him as a playboy if you didn't know anything about him. He throws his money around, pays for all my drinks, and gives waiters unnecessarily large tips. I had a hunch there was a lot more to him than appears. He didn't seem to be a happy man though he laughed a lot, and he talked about never having done anything in his life worth while. That's what he said on the first night as the *Aquitania* was foghorning its way into Cherbourg.

But yesterday it was a different Tim Mayfield. After dinner, as we were sipping brandy, he showed me two letters . . . the most remarkable documents I have ever seen.

One was from Anthony Eden written on the day he resigned. It was written in terms of extraordinary affection on Foreign Office writing paper and in Eden's own handwriting, and it was obvious from the tone of the letter that Eden had discussed at length with Tim the question of his resignation. The other was from Ramsay MacDonald at the time he was Prime Minister. The letter was even more remarkable than Eden's. There was a whole page describing Tim in superlatives and showing that Tim had been a Secret Service officer of exceptional importance. As I read it I remembered a phrase in Eden's letter: 'MacDonald always said you were a dreamer.'

He has hidden all those achievements from me till now. Nor did he tell me till later that he had been one of Lawrence of Arabia's greatest friends, and that Lawrence sent for him on his deathbed, and that he had given Tim a special copy of *The Mint*.

So it has turned out that my voyage across the Atlantic has been a fascinating one.

I saw him from time to time in New York, and on one occasion he invited me to go to Toronto for a few days as his guest, and this I did. As usual he was lavishly hospitable. Not for a moment did I ever have a reason to be suspicious as to where the money came from.

I continued my world tour, and I did not see him again until after the war. Then one evening I was at an elegant cocktail party in an apartment in Belgrave Square when suddenly I saw Tim, a beautiful young woman beside him. He caught my eye, paused for a moment, then, when another guest began talking to his companion, threaded his way across the room to me.

'Hello, Derek,' he said, then he whispered to me urgently, 'you won't let on, will you?'

I had had very happy times in his company, and he had become a friend. Since I was a boy I have believed if you have someone whom you can call a friend, loyalty to that friend is sacrosant. Never betray a friend, I thought, and will always think so.

Thus there was no chance that I should betray Tim.

You see, in the interval between saying goodbye to him in New York and this moment at the cocktail party in Belgrave Square, I had received one letter from him, and the address at the top of the notepaper, a lengthy number below it, was Parkhurst Prison, Isle of Wight.

Tim had been convicted as a confidence trickster, a charming, delightful, convincing confidence trickster. He certainly deceived me, but it was a very pleasant deception. It was another milestone in my education, the education which helps to mature a young man who is seeking experience from a world tour.

I continued to finger through the diary of my New York days, and I came to the date which began a saga that, years later, was to end in disaster. Its beginning, however, was delightful. It was an example of another experience which a young man on a world tour looks for.

July 7th.

I've met a lovely girl called Sarah. She was the understudy to Claire Luce in John Steinbeck's *Of Mice and Men*, and she is now the ingénue lead in a very successful play on Broadway.

The other night I got back to the Algonquin around midnight when I saw this lovely thing exercising a white Persian cat on a lead outside the hotel, up and down the pavement. The girl was slim with natural fair hair falling down over her shoulders. I walked up to her and saw her lovely splash of a mouth, and she looked at me and the vibes had begun operating.

I looked at the white Persian cat which she held on the lead and realized, although I hate cats, I must make this cat my friend. The cat was my passport to the girl, and so when I reached the two of them I made my overtures to the cat not to the girl. As I did so, the girl murmured something to me, then turned and led the cat into the Algonquin. I followed . . . then one thing led to another, and the cat was put to bed and the girl and I were soon at the bar introducing ourselves to each other. We seemed to have so many thoughts and attitudes in common. I'm now going to bed, aware that my time in New York is going to be exciting.

July 10th.

I've left the Algonquin and gone to the Royalton on the other side of 44th Street. Sarah suggested it, saying that we would be freer if we were not in the same hotel where people would be watching us. Today I took her out to lunch. I had already arranged to meet Russell Swann, the magician, whom I had written about in my London column. I had thought him brilliant, and on this occasion he didn't disappoint me . . . and by his presence, talking to Sarah about the influence of my column, enhanced me in her eyes. And he achieved this in one quite amazing way. I told Russell I had changed my hotel, and now had a lovely room with a balcony overlooking the skyline of New York. With hardly a moment's hesitation he exclaimed: 'I know, I know! It's on the fourteenth floor and the number is 1416!' And he was correct.

July 14th.

Ted Husing is the best known sports and radio commentator in the States. Yesterday Sarah and I were in the Waldorf when he came up to us. Sarah was overwhelmed. He started asking us questions, and when he found that I was a London columnist on a world tour, he said he would like to have me on his show and would we now come and have supper with him at Twenty-One, the prestigious club which only accepts the top people of the time. Of course we said yes . . . and soon we found ourselves sitting at a table with Paul Whiteman,

Harry Richman, and two of the top New York columnists. Ted Husing, introducing us to Paul Whiteman, said,
'Everyone loves Paul. He treats his musicians as part of a
family, pays them extravagantly, and cares for the family of
any one of them who might become ill.' Having had supper
he took us to Columbia Studios for his midnight broadcast
and proceeded to introduce me, saying he had a famous British newspaper columnist as his special guest. Connie Boswell
was in the programme. She was wheeled in and once on stage,
by some miracle, she jumped up from her wheelchair, stood
normally and began to sing. Sarah was impressed by all this.

July 20th.

Sarah is deliciously naive. I paid too much attention to a
girl at a party, and I felt Sarah sitting frigid beside me.
Afterwards she said: 'Derek, I had such a funny feeling, a
feeling I've never had before, that of jealousy. I always
wanted to feel it, and though I hate you for giving a line to
that girl, I loved you for making me jealous.'

July 21st.

I sent flowers this afternoon to her at the theatre, and
before the evening performance was over a note had been
delivered to me at the Royalton. 'You seem almost like a
dream to me. I can hardly realize that these past three weeks
have actually been as they were. It was all so quick and
sudden. Please don't see me tomorrow. I want to be calm
and see things in perspective . . .'

August 3rd.

Of course she is very, very pretty, and very intelligent.
She is only twenty-two, and although her career is in the

theatre, she also writes, and she has had a short story published in the *Saturday Evening Post*. She was eighteen when she came to New York to realize her ambition to break into the theatrical world. She earned a living for the first six months as a dance hostess in a nightclub. Then one day she had the luck of being spotted by a well-known producer as she was walking down 43rd Street 'When the best pair of legs in New York walked past my theatre,' said the man, who was the famous Earl Carroll, 'I stop them.' Ten minutes later she had a job as a chorus girl.

August 10th.

I've suddenly made up my mind to leave New York, and take a Greyhound bus across the States to San Francisco. There was much emotion when I told Sarah. I pointed out a paragraph in Danton Walker's Broadway column which had triggered my decision: 'Derek Tangye, twenty-six-year-old London columnist, who is doing a round the world reporting job, can't tear himself away from New York on account of a gal in *Bachelor Born*.' It jerked me. I had such a long way to go. My time with Sarah must end.

August 14th.

I left New York two days ago. I was leaving in the evening at half past eight. We went shopping in the afternoon, and we had an irresponsible time, much laughter and the understanding of easy companionship. We said goodbye at half past seven in my room. I was packing and she lay on my bed and chaffed me. It was all so easy and so much fun. Then it was time for her to go to the theatre, and I was alone. Just before she left, she handed me an envelope. 'Open it at midnight,' she said. This I did as I sat in the Greyhound bus as it careered across New York State. Here it is:

> Please don't be angry with me. I'm giving you this instead of a cigarette lighter or some other silly thing you'd have no use for. Every bit helps, and I'm sure you can use it. Besides it's very easy to carry. If you send it back to me, I'll sleep with the first man I can find. Have your adventures and if you get into any real trouble please wire me because if I am in work I can send you enough to get you back here. Regardless how you feel, you've made me very happy. Please come back one day. I will never forget you.

She had enclosed a ten-dollar bill.

We kept in touch during my travels, and we were in touch during the war years. When I married Jeannie, Sarah, because it was clothes-ration time and she had the same slim figure as Jeannie, would send Jeannie clothes she no longer needed. She married an English stage and film director who lived in the States soon after the end of the war and they came to London for their honeymoon. One night, I remember, they were our guests in the Savoy Restaurant, and the four of us were witnesses of a charming incident concerning Princess Margaret. Princess Elizabeth, as she was then, had a special table away from the dance floor whenever she went to the Savoy, and on this occasion, when the evening was ending, she tried to attract the attention of her younger sister to tell her that it was time to go. Our table was adjacent to the dance floor and we were amused by Princess Margaret's tactics. She was dancing with a tall man, making her look very diminutive, and we heard her say as she passed our table: 'Please keep dancing with your back to my sister so that I can't see her!'

During her stay, Sarah wanted me to show her around London, and this I did, finding that she knew more about the historic areas like the Tower of London than I did. It was pleasant to do so, but I felt no emotion. New York was a long, long time away. It happens like that sometimes. You want to respond to someone who loves you, but you are stopped by an invisible barrier. Jeannie, meanwhile, was amused, just as I was amused observing her being pursued by one film star after another. I was flattered that I had a young wife who was so bewitching, and happy that we both knew we had a harbour to which we could safely return.

Neither of us, however, was to be happy after the next visit of Sarah and her husband. We had moved to Cornwall and had begun our primitive life at Minack, struggling to develop a market garden, when Sarah and her husband announced they were coming to Cornwall to see us and could we find somewhere near where they could stay? We found a farmhouse, and told them they could have their meals with us. We had no running water, no electricity, and our daily life was filled with earthy tasks. Their visit passed off normally – more or less normally, I should perhaps say. The consequences, however, were very abnormal.

A year later we had a letter to say that Sarah had written a play about the visit. We were mildly amused, thinking that it would be a comedy, a Nöel Coward type of thing with the theme of what happens when two Americans visit an English couple living in primitive circumstances. The play opened in the then St James's Theatre. We had alerted my mother and friends, and they took tickets for the first night. We ourselves mooched through the evening with Monty our cat, scarcely thinking of the events three hundred miles away in the West End of London, too concerned with planning the labouring activities of the morrow. But the morrow proved to be sensational.

At four p.m. my cousin Carol arrived in his car. Half an hour later Prince Chula of Thailand, an old friend who had a house near Bodmin, also arrived. They both brought the same message. They had been at the first night, and felt so enraged by what they witnessed on the stage that, in loyalty to us, they were impelled to drive all the way from London to warn us. The set of the play, they told us, was identical to the interior of our cottage. The scenes depicted a mockery of our lives. There were so many incidents that could identify us as the couple who had left the glitter lights for a hopeful, peaceful time in Cornwall that they urged us to take legal action forthwith.

We did so, and after the expected legal wrangle the play was withdrawn and we received financial damages. We accepted £2000. Not much compared to the hurt it had done to our confidence in people, but it was enough to pay for the pump which we had been unable to buy and which would draw water from the thirty-foot well we had sunk . . . and to enable us to have running water and a bath for the first time in the cottage.

There was, understandably, silence between Sarah, her husband and ourselves for a long while afterwards. Then Sarah's husband died after a long illness. Then she heard that Jeannie had died, and a few weeks afterwards she wrote to me suggesting I should come to New York. This, of course, I ignored. Yet her continued attention intrigued me. Here was an example of the grey area of life, the area which theorists, or a computer, are unable to cater for. It is an area where opposites reign, and no conclusive decision is realized.

A time came when a decision had to be made. Four years after Jeannie had died Sarah wrote to say that she was coming to Cornwall to see me. I was horrified. I had no wish to see her, but she said she was determined to come and she gave me the date and time of her arrival at Penzance. I foresaw disaster, but there was such a determined sound in her letter that I knew I could not stop her. And it was a disaster.

I met her at Penzance Station, and there emerged this sophisticated lady, so far away in my memory of a very pretty twenty-two-year-old challenging the excitement of life. When we arrived back at the cottage which I loved so much, I found it being compared with her Park Avenue apartment. There began, during her three-day stay, the language of all the reasons why Jeannie and I left London to escape . . . not just the language but also the behaviour.

It was a disaster for both of us. 'I'll never come to Cornwall again,' she wrote a few days later; and on each of the three days of her stay I scrawled on an otherwise empty page of my diary: 'Don't want to remember today.'

An odd thing happened on the morning after she left. I opened the suitcase which had been my original objective before I became diverted by the travel diary, and began rummaging through the contents . . . and suddenly I put my hands on a battered envelope. It was the envelope which had contained the ten-dollar bill she had given me that evening when I left New York in a Greyhound bus. A bittersweet ending to a story which began when I saw a girl with fair hair falling down over her shoulders exercising a white Persian cat on a lead outside the Algonquin Hotel on 44th Street.

Cats, although I grew up to hate them, were to become a dominant influence in my life. I came from a dog-loving family, and cats were considered vermin. First, however, there was the white Persian cat of 44th Street, then came Monty whom I first saw gambolling on the floor of Jeannie's office in Room 205 of the Savoy Hotel. Monty the kitten the colour of autumn bracken was the key which changed my attitude, although the change took place slowly. For instance, when Jeannie asked me to take him home to Mortlake in a basket, I mockingly threatened I would throw him over Hammersmith Bridge. But as the years went by Monty captured my heart, and others followed him: Lama, Oliver, Ambrose . . . and Cherry, who was at that moment sitting on my lap purring and making it difficult for me to write. Each I have loved unashamedly.

I had, however, once put into print my attitude towards cats. It was in an article which I now found in the suitcase, an article that was to change the course of my life and the most important one I was ever to write though I had no clue about this at the time. A magazine asked me to write about my likes and dislikes. It was read by the *Daily Mirror* management who were looking for a replacement for the legendary Godfrey Winn who was moving to another newspaper. The management liked the article, sent for me and I was offered Godfrey Winn's place. As a result I became a celebrity overnight. The hype buzzed around me. My photograph was on London buses, queues of girls rushed after me if they saw me in the street, and I was once embarrassingly mobbed when I made a publicity appearance in the Hammersmith Palais de Danse. But what of the article which prompted all this?

Having listed my likes and dislikes, I ended with a flourish. I had reserved to the last paragraph of my article, which I was now holding in my hand with Cherry purring on my lap, my major dislike.

'Above all,' I exclaimed, 'I dislike cats!'

VII

There was no chance of Jeannie and me separating during our married life, even if we had wished to do so. Monty, Lama, Oliver, Ambrose, Cherry bound us together. Who, for instance, would have the custody of the cat?

As I continued to dip my hands into the suitcase, I confronted evidence of the tapestry which kept us together. There is no logical code which did so. We were blessed by the intangible driving force of being able to share each other's lives. I am unable to believe that rules, as mirrored by marriage counsellors, can provide the base of a happy marriage. One has, for example, a Royal lady as President of Relate, the marriage guidance organization, who was unable to solve the problems of her own marriage. Counsellors may be able to smooth over jagged edges, help a couple through a bad patch, but they can only provide a temporary, superficial solution. A happy marriage, a fundamentally happy marriage, is based on a string of unorganized emotions which cannot be defined in logical language. Jeannie and I had rows, but they were only the eruption of bad temper. They never simmered. 'Aren't we lucky?' Jeannie used to say at intervals all her life.

We were in tune, for instance, as to what we wanted out of life. We both wanted success when we were young, and we both achieved it. I as a columnist and as a result of my first three books, Jeannie as the legendary publicity girl of the Savoy Hotel Group. We had each begun our lives in London without knowing a soul, yet proceeded to become close friends with those who had been our heroes and heroines. But once we had experienced this success, we both came to the conclusion that we had no wish indefinitely to maintain it. We wanted to change direction when we still had time to begin a new life. We wanted to be free. We wanted to avoid being slaves of big corporations. Thus we came to Minack; and from the moment we made our home on this wild Cornish coast there was not an instant when we wanted to leave it. Here again was an example of that 'intangible driving force of being able to share each other's lives'. Jeannie's friends and colleagues never expected 'the prettiest publicity girl in the world' to cope with such a primitive life. They waited for her to fail, waited for her to return to the sophisticated merry-go-round. They waited hopefully for her to fail . . . hopefully because they wanted reassurance that their own way of life was the right one. But Jeannie did not fail. There was never a moment when there was any prospect of her failing.

When such a union as ours is severed, the tears are there but one must not show them; and always there remains in my mind that remark of the Queen Mother when asked how she carried on with her public duties, smiling at the crowds, after King George VI had died: 'You should see me in my private moments.'

I have found, however, reasons for rejoicing that I am the one who was left. I rejoice because I could care for Jeannie until she died. I rejoice because I was the one who had to face up to the details, the awesome details, that followed. I rejoice because I was the one who had to face up to the hiatus of being alone. Jeannie was spared all this, spared the burden of readjustment. I feel I am repaying her love over the years.

I picked up a letter from my mother from the suit-case. She had written it a couple of weeks before our wedding. We were to be married at Richmond Church and the reception was to be held at my then home, Cholmondely House, Friars Lane, a beautiful Regency house with bow windows looking over the towpath and the Thames. The letter was in reply to a request by Jeannie. Fond as she was of her own mother, Jeannie wanted my mother to be the one to help her in the pre-wedding organizing. My mother called Jeannie 'a pocket Venus', and they were devoted to each other from the time I first introduced them. My mother was so easy with young people that they all felt they were of the same age group. She, though having a flat in London, spent much of her time with my father at Glendorgal, the family home in Cornwall.

Here is the letter to Jeannie.

Darling, *what* a lovely letter to receive . . . it is so wonderful to know that one is *wanted*. You gave such interesting details too, bless you. I'm thrilled with it all, and as you know I adore listening to plans and talking them over, and being practical. I shall adore to come . . . it is my beloved Gib I have to think about. I know that he will be utterly unselfish about it, but I do worry about him. I'm so glad you've fixed up with Mrs Benson, but do fix up definitely that she does your laundry and mends things and darns socks and so on. It is much better to have it all quite clear from the beginning.

Alongside my mother's letter in the suitcase was a collection of other nostalgic ones. There was, for instance, the letter Jeannie had written to me on the day of the wedding, sending it by special delivery to Cholmondely House before the ceremony at 12.15.

My darling, how are you feeling? I am so happy this morning, exquisitely happy because I am going to be Mrs Derek Tangye. I hope I will always make you as happy as you have made me . . . which is happier than I ever thought anyone could be. My love is for you always.

And there was the last letter she ever wrote to me.

My darling, today you have just given me the introduction to *The Cherry Tree*, and I am so very happy. It is all I could ever want and I feel so proud to have been able to be such a part of it and of all the effort and love put into it. I am a very lucky girl to have your wonderful love and I shall treasure it forever.

She was my partner in all my books, just as I was a partner in hers. I did not know her when I wrote my first book *Time was Mine*, but it was the reason I met her. I went to the Savoy Hotel and asked her to put the book prominently on the bookstall. Then followed a time when she helped me gather the stories for *Went the Day Well*, and she was at my side, encouraging me, when I was involved in the mammoth task of writing my survey of the British Commonwealth called *One King*. Then came the Minack Chronicles, and she was the heroine, inspiring me over the years. I, in my turn, helped her with *Meet Me at the Savoy* and her hotel novels, *Hotel Regina, Home is the Hotel* and *Bertioni's Hotel*. We shared the struggle, the frustrations, the disappointments, the successes; and all the while working with our hands in the soil, we shared another form of struggle, frustration, disappointment and success.

Jeannie was the first to write a book after we came to Minack. My part in the sharing was to behave like a schoolmaster, disciplining her. I knew from experience that no book is ever written without self-discipline on the part of the author, and such self-discipline is hard to impose upon oneself. One can very easily find something else to do, and Jeannie was skilled in so doing. Thus I devised a routine in which I persuaded her to go into the spare room, which was a hut adjacent to the cottage, and then lock her in it. Someone calling would ask 'Where is Jeannie?', and I would reply that I had locked her out of sight. They would mockingly call me cruel, but when *Meet Me at the Savoy* was at last published they were full of praise for my cruelty.

There were reviews of *Meet Me at the Savoy* in the suitcase, fascinating reviews, the more fascinating since several publishers had turned the book down. Here is a review from a national magazine:

Meet Me at the Savoy is a gossipy, glamorous true story about a great hotel, the important people who frequent it, and perhaps the even more important people behind the scenes who cater for their comforts.

For ten years Jean Nicol was public relations officer to the Savoy Hotel Group, the Savoy, the Berkeley, and Claridge's ... but she writes mainly about the Savoy where she had her headquarters. A procession of notabilities marches and trips through the pages of the book, and what a procession! Royal personages, statesmen, stars of stage and screen, authors, journalists, many of them American. Jean Nicol tells us about them all, intimately but never indiscreetly, and most of them she writes about as friends.

Her job, of course, was to get publicity, the right kind of publicity. This, though she never boasts about it, she must have performed very successfully, for it is clear she loved the Savoy and liked people, all sorts of people, and it is my guess that she twisted most of them around her little finger. A vital, fascinating book.

There was a copy of the *Savoy Standard* in the suitcase. Now such a copy is a collector's piece. It was created in the early war years when American correspondents flooded into the Savoy, making it their London headquarters.

The first idea for it came from Bob Post of the *New York Times*. 'Jeannie,' he said to her one morning, 'I've got a wonderful idea. Why don't you get all the American war correspondents staying in the hotel to write a Savoy newspaper? You can edit it, and you'll get wonderful publicity. Besides, it will be great fun.'

Jeannie became the editor, and she had all the head-aches of an editor, though she also greatly enjoyed it. The correspondents worshipped her, and it was fascinating to watch her handle them. There was no need for a harassment act to protect her. There was no need for her to moan for equal rights. Her femininity made her the boss.

The aftermath was a sad one. Bob Post, a solemn, desk-bound type of journalist won a coveted place in the rota of American journalists selected to go on bombing raids. He came to Jeannie's office, Room 205, one day, and Jeannie sensed that something was wrong. 'You look depressed, Bob,' she said. 'Well, not exactly,' he replied slowly, 'but you know how all the boys are raring to go on a bombing raid over Germany . . . well, they have picked another lot today and I am one of them. It isn't that I don't want to go.' He paused, and looked out of the window. 'You see, Jeannie. I know that I am not coming back.'

And he never did.

There was a letter which showed what the American correspondents thought of Jeannie. It came from a senior executive of Hearst Newspapers, John Brogan. It had been sent to Jeannie after it had been announced that she was leaving the Savoy.

So you've bought a castle in Cornwall and are going to settle down to the quiet lady in country life! Well, you probably have ambitions to write just like Derek, and you probably will write, but London isn't ever going to be the same without you, and certainly not the Savoy Hotel. The Savoy could throw all the glittering French ornaments and Louis XV furniture into the Thames as long as it kept Jean Nicol Tangye as an ornament . . . wherever you are and whatever you do, Jeannie, a big bundle of love from this old walrus. God bless.

We had another form of sharing. A couple each with separate jobs meets each other after work and asks: 'Did you have a good day?' Neither is aware of the office clashes of the other. Neither of them is aware of the weaving problems that affect the other. For a dozen hours they have lived separate lives, and that separation doesn't end there. In the early hours of the morning they may be lying together, but each, lying disturbingly awake, is worrying about problems the other knows nothing about.

This is where Jeannie and I were so lucky. Our careers merged into one. It had been so since we had first met. Jeannie mixed with the same people that I needed to mix with. When she was called up, summoned to the Denmark Street recruiting office and told that she was being directed into the khaki uniform of the ATS, she exclaimed to a disapproving lady behind the desk: 'Oh but I hate the uniform. I want to join the Wrens who wear black stockings!' But she wasn't going to join either. She had now become an agent for MI5. Her presence in the Savoy was far too precious for MI5, MI6 and the Secretary of the War Cabinet for her to be shuttled into the anonymity of the armed services. Thus I intervened. Thus a directive came down to Denmark Street from my chief that Jean Nicol should remain at the Savoy. No hint was given that I had been the mastermind. Indeed the story was sent around, deliberately, that it was the influence of Hugh Wontner, Chairman of the Savoy, who had achieved this freedom for Jeannie.

We had so much to share together. We shared the hazards of an author on the way to publication. We shared the moments, after a few hours writing, of being disgusted by what we had written. We shared moments of despair. We shared the glorious moment when one of us had finished a chapter and nervously handed it to the other for their opinion . . . then erupting with happiness when the other said that the chapter was brilliant. Each of us, in our sharing, tried to boost the morale of the other.

We shared the rejection slips, and the doubting phrases of literary agents whom one believes at the outset of a book-publishing journey are infallible. Of *A Gull on the Roof* my then literary agent sent me a letter: 'I have had a couple of reports on *A Gull on the Roof*, which I regret to say are not as enthusiastic as I had hoped. But I will keep trying.' Jeannie received a comment from the literary agent to whom she had sent the first of her three hotel novels, *Hotel Regina*, and the man starkly replied, 'It is unpublishable!' It is one of the strangest quirks of the book trade that a literary agent may continue to collect his ten per cent for ever. An author may not have had anything to do with him for thirty years, but in the event of any subsidiary rights of the book being sold the literary agent still collects his ten per cent although he had nothing to do with the selling.

Then, in the suitcase, were echoes of our early years of Minack sharing. I found two letters from Tommy Williams, the gaunt, mystical, tall Cornishman who was the first person to help us, and who started to do so before we came permanently to live at Minack. He would send us letters reporting what he had been doing. He was clearing, for instance, the undergrowth around the cottage, and beginning to open up the cliff meadows.

Here in my hand were these crumpled letters written in spidery handwriting. How excited we were when we first received them, thrilled by the tangible evidence of the life we were going to lead.

I am pleased to inform you that I have trimmed down all the hedges round top and bottom. I have burned the trimmings and been around the field hedges and put back all small stones. I have cut the trees back around the two home meadows and stacked branches around the hedges to keep out cattle. The little potato house meadow will be a nice meadow when I've finished breaking it . . . Well, that is all for the present. Tommy Williams.

The second letter:

I've put away 10 cwt of Pilot potato seed, and will put away

101

10 cwt of Homeguard next week. If the weather is kind they should shoot quite early, and if all goes well when we plant them, and I'll start doing that in the first week of February, we can hope for a good early crop, and we will have the advantage of growing them in ground which has never grown potatoes before.

I will leave the suitcase for a moment because I found our first Minack logbook in Labour Warms, and that logbook is so much a part of Tommy Williams. He was our mainstay at the beginning. Loyal, hardworking, eccentric, he was just the person to bridge our sophisticated life with our rough, new one. He seemed to be part of the rocks, the soil, the wild daffodils, the gorse, the bracken, and the birds and the foxes and the badgers. He lived alone in a caravan a mile away. It seemed inconceivable that he would ever want to leave an environment in which his forebears had lived for generations and in which he himself was entrenched. But something in his mind was nagging away at him . . . and there came a day when he startled us by informing us he was leaving the district. 'Why? Where are you going, Tommy?' I had asked. His reply, the motive behind the reply, was incomprehensible. He had applied for a job in Birmingham Parks, and he had secured it. Birmingham Parks! I remember reacting with astonishment. Tommy, who seemed to be a human being as wild as a badger, heading for a life in Birmingham Parks! Well, he left the Cornish cliffs, settled in Birmingham and died there.

I will always remember him with his telescope. He might be planting potatoes, he might be digging new potatoes, but if he saw a ship in the vast area of Mount's Bay which he did not recognize, his work had to stop, the telescope be produced and the staring begin. He also liked to have mocking jokes at the *Scillonian* as she passed us to and from the Islands, especially if it was bad weather. 'I'm glad I'm not on board,' he would say, roaring with laughter.

Here are excerpts from the logbook, and the kind of world he left. It was our first year at Minack, the first account of how Jeannie and I set out to share a new adventure.

April 8th . . . Arrived at last. Hens laid six eggs on the journey down in the Land-Rover! Odd items I have learnt . . . potatoes are locally called taties . . . 25 cwt of seed potatoes go to the acre . . . expect hopefully four to one return on earlies, and expect to draw cliff meadows second week in May . . . if there is a frost at night, it is the sun which will turn the potato leaves black if it is shining in the morning.

May 10th . . . Our first potato harvest has begun! For the past few days we have been becoming increasingly excited. We have been going down the cliff, fingering in the soil, and were so disappointed to find the potatoes we fingered were the size of marbles. Tommy says we must wait for rain to make them swell, but we amateurs have proved the professional wrong. This morning Jeannie got thoroughly impatient. I was cautious. I was on Tommy's side. 'Don't be a coward,' said Jeannie. 'Come on, let's go to the bottom meadow by the sea, and have a try there.' I collected the long-handled shovel, Jeannie carried a bundle of chips, and we went down the cliff. Jeannie was right! By lunchtime we had dug 2 top-grade chips, and 1 mid. Had some for supper. *So* delicious. The flavour of the real Cornish new potato.

May 22nd . . . We are in full swing. Blissful weather and we were down the cliff soon after dawn. Sheer ecstasy. We were on another planet. By the end of the day we had 23 graded chips, 2 mids. Don't understand why they are called mids, these thumbnail size potatoes.

May 24th . . . It really is a good crop. Sent away 59 graded, 5 mids, all to Daniel's of Birmingham. All this week 7d a lb clear.

May 29th . . . The farmers have begun in the fields, the price is dropping daily, and we have switched to bags. But we can't complain, we have now sent away 174 chips, each holding 14 lbs, and all these chips have been carried up the cliff by Tommy and me. Exhausting. Then Jeannie was in charge of weighing them at the bottom of the big field. Then we packed them into the Land-Rover, and I drove straight to Penzance Station.

June 16th . . . All the week we have been digging the top half of the big field, much easier working, all going in bags . . . just have had great news that foreign imports have stopped, and both Lincolnshire and Pembrokeshire have bad crops. Prices have rocketed, but we have nearly finished. Never mind. We are really pleased with our first effort at potato growing.

The logbook reported other activities.

June 23rd . . . We have planted 4000 Governor Herrick violets in the big field, did so as soon as we had finished the potatoes. We have had a disaster with 1000 Princess of Wales violets we planted three weeks ago. They have been decimated by rabbits.

July 1st . . . Planted 1000 wallflower plants, and we have also sown 12,000 anemone corms, and planted 500 polyanthus, the special blue variety from Blackmore and Langdon of Bath.

August 14th . . . I put down a lobster pot in our little bay for the first time, and have caught a conger! Jeannie was scared by the sight of it when I brought it to her in the kitchen!

September 1st . . . We have started planting daffodil bulbs, 2 cwt of Soleil D'Or so far, then we have 5 cwt of King Alfred to plant. We are on our way to become daffodil growers.

There were sweet, innocent moments also recorded in the logbook, moments that captured the wonder of the life we had begun to live.

September 4th . . . John Chappell, the old water diviner from Treen, has been here today, trying to find an underground spring for a well to give us a water supply instead of catching rainwater. He kept us fascinated with local folklore stories.

For instance he told us if you put tar outside a fox's earth or a rat hole, it will drive them away; and a fox gets rid of its fleas by holding a tuft of its fur in its mouth and standing in a stream. When the tuft is full of fleas it lets it go; and if a fox is chasing a chicken, and the chicken is smart enough to fly up a tree, the fox will hypnotize it into coming down by walking round and round in circles beneath the tree. We took it all very seriously. Only later did we realize that John Chappel was just humouring us, just entertaining two newly arrived ex-city dwellers.

And there is the description in the logbook of our first threshing day. Farmers in the district shared their workforce when each had their threshing day in August, and there was always rivalry between the farmers' wives as to who would provide the best midday meal of the season.

August 22nd . . . We have been helping out with the threshing at the Ellis farm at the top of the lane, and here are some notes I have made of my impressions . . . the noise of the engine of the combine harvester, the chaff flying in the breeze, the small boy with his mock bag of corn, the little girl crying when told she had to go home, the laughter and goodwill of all those who were working, the faded red shafts of the cart and the grey horse pulling it, the men high on the stack, silhouetted against the deep blue sky, each standing poised to await another bundle of straw to be tossed to them, the sea in the distance and the soft breeze, the mouse running through the straw, the anxious Mrs Ellis, anxious about the midday meal she will soon be providing, anxious as to how it would be compared with that of her neighbours. We've had such a beautiful day.

I returned to the suitcase and picked out the census records of the nineteenth century, records of those who had lived where Jeannie and I lived. People who had touched the rocks that we touched, who looked up at the granite chimney we looked at, who worked the fields which we had worked, who left their intangible impressions on this land which became our home. 'How long have you been here?' visitors will often ask, and I reply that we arrived yesterday. Some are nonplussed by my reply, others understand that this is a timeless place, as timeless as the rocks around the cottage, as timeless as the granite slabs in the cottage walls. And I think of those people who lived here, who were part of a long-ago history . . . the French Revolutions, the American War of Independence, the antics of the Georges and the Prince Regent, the Battle of Trafalgar, the young Victoria being crowned Queen, the spread of the British Empire, Queen Victoria dying, all the multitude of historical events. What was the reaction of the inhabitants of Minack to this? Theirs was an age when people were not saturated with news and instant opinions. They mirror the saying which Jeannie loved to quote: 'To be happy, never go beyond the garden gate.'

Who were these people who lived at Minack in the nineteenth century, and whose active lives in the land around us had been obliterated by time? The census records their names, and they also give an explanation for misunderstandings which have existed to this day. Note that on four occasions the cottage is listed as 'Minack', on the fifth occasion as 'Dorminac'.

MINACK 1841: Peter Ellis, aged 30, Jennifer Ellis, 27, Grace, 6, Isabella, 4, Charles, 1. Peter Ellis is described as agricultural labourer.

MINACK 1851: Richard Botheras, aged 27, Mary Botheras, 24, William Botheras, 5 months.

DORMINAC 1861: Thomas Watters, 38, Catherine Watters, 40, Henry, 6, Thomas, 4, Elizabeth, 2. Thomas Watters described as dairyman.

MINACK 1871: Eli Trewern, 28, Mary Jane Trewern, 26, Grace, 1.

MINACK 1881: Eli Trewern, 38, Mary Jane Trewern, 36, Grace, 11, Annie, 10, Elizabeth, 8.

In the twentieth century the cottage became Dormi-nack. Why? Minack is the Cornish for stony, Dor for home or place; and the official address today is Dorminack.

When Jeannie and I came to the cottage, locals – and old ones still do – referred to the cottage as Minack (the *i* as in *y*). 'How is it down Minack?' someone would ask. Or: 'Don't you feel it lonely down Minack?'

I had written three of the Minack Chronicles, includ-ing *A Gull on the Roof*, *A Cat in the Window*, and *A Drake at the Door*, when the open air theatre situated on the cliffs a few miles away changed its name to the Minack Theatre (pronounced Minnack), and all the direction signs in the neighbourhood were changed from 'To the Open Air Theatre' to 'To the Minack Theatre'. I remember the moment when we first had news of the change. A group of early followers of the Chronicles arrived. 'We are confused! We saw these signs, followed them, yet saying it doesn't seem feasible that the Tangyes are advertising themselves in such a way.'

A muddled situation, therefore, and it became more, muddled. Captain Warwick, the captain of the *QE 2* had written to us saying that he enjoyed the Chronicles, and he would like to see where we lived . . . but he would have to bring the *QE 2* along with him. Needless to say we were startled and thrilled by such a proposal. Punctually at the appointed time of five o'clock the *QE 2* arrived, slowly sailing past a mile offshore, close enough for us to see the cameras of the passengers who were crowding the rails, pointing towards us.

The Cornwall Tourist Board decided to take advantage of the occasion. An aircraft flew overhead, low down, with press photographers aboard, and there were other photographers standing in the field which has been known ever since as the *QE 2* field. Penny and Fred, the donkeys, were also there. The *QE 2* sounded her sirens in greeting and Penny and Fred replied with a cascade of bewildered hee-haws. There was much publicity on television and in the national press, and this did not please everyone. The then manager of the open air theatre – now called the Minack Theatre – was one of them. In a letter he requested that I should stop using the name Minack, and that if I did he would remove the effigy of me on his mantelpiece in which he stuck pins.

How should I react? I replied jokingly. 'Let's discuss the matter,' I wrote. 'Why not come over here and I'll

try to stop the donkeys from kicking you over the cliff!'
He never came, but the remarkable Rowena Cade, who
founded and built the theatre, was to write a charming
letter and all was well. It is a wonderful theatre; go
there if you ever have a chance. It will be an unforgettable experience.

My mind went back to the lives of the previous inhabitants of Minack: the Ellis family, the Botheras family,
the Watters family, the Trewern family . . . their ghosts
were around me. They lived in times when nature still
dominated the world, and cities were in concentrated
units, when roads and lanes were winding, when there
were no threats of planners destroying the countryside
one had known all one's life, when there was no over-
population, when migrating birds could return year
after year to nesting sites which had been left undisturbed, when badgers were safe from bulldozers obliter-
ating their setts, when rivers were unpolluted, when
simple pleasures reigned in villages, when there was no
lure to stare mindlessly at a television screen, when the
media respected privacy, when all over the world beautiful places were unspoilt by developers. I remembered
a letter, a copy of which had been sent to me. It was
from the chief of an Indian tribe to the President of
the United States in 1855. The president had notified
the chief of the Duwanish Indians in Washington
State that it was intended to buy their land for white
settlers. The copy of the chief's letter had been sent to
me by Ann Schwengels, an air stewardess with United
Airlines based in San Francisco. She had paid a visit to

Minack and had become a follower of the Minack Chronicles. 'It is a way,' she said, 'of saying thank you.' The letter is as follows:

The Great Chief in Washington sends word that he wishes to buy our land. How can you buy or sell the sky, the warmth of the land? The idea is strange to us. We do not own the freshness of the air or the sparkle of the water. How can you buy them from us? Every part of this earth is sacred to my people. Every shiny pine needle, every sandy shore, every mist in the dark woods, every clearing, and every humming insect is holy in the memory and experience of my people.

We knew that white man does not understand our ways. One portion of the land is the same to him as the next, for he is a stranger who comes in the night and takes from the land whatever he needs. The earth is not his brother but his enemy, and when he has conquered it he moves on. He leaves his father's grave, his children's birthright is forgotten.

There is no quiet place in the white man's cities. No place to hear the leaves of spring or the rustle of insect wings. But perhaps I am a savage and do not understand because the clatter only seems to insult the ears. Yet what is there to life if a man cannot hear the lovely cry of a curlew or the sound of a frog around the pond at night?

And all the while, all the while that I had been rummaging through the suitcase, the back of my mind had been simmering with the question: who was growing the cannabis down our cliff?

VIII

Two close friends who were on holiday in the area came to visit me at the beginning of April. I was glad to see them. I was feeling vulnerable. I needed someone I could trust, someone with whom I could frankly discuss every aspect of my cannabis worries. I told them all I knew . . . and the outcome was that they volunteered to become undercover agents on my behalf. They would tour the local pubs, become friendly with those present and try to infiltrate the local drug scene.

During the weeks leading up to this time I had been in two minds as to whether I should keep the discovery of the cannabis secret, or let it be known generally. In the beginning I did indeed keep it secret. Perhaps my reason was sentimental, a kind of protection against the horrific knowledge that the bulbs which grew in the meadows were now in a strange, uncouth place, gazed upon by the thief who planted the cannabis in their place. The same sentimental reason, I realized, why I couldn't persuade myself to go and see for myself the evidence of the theft. It hurt too much to remember the hours that Jeannie and myself had sat there, innocently happy that we lived in a Minack world of honesty.

112

But when no clues developed as to who was the cause of my distress, I realized it would be sensible to circulate the story, thus involving all sorts of people who might lead to a line of investigation. Yet still no clues emerged. This seemed so strange. True, there were some strong opinions expressed as to who the culprit might be but such opinions, I found, were based on personal prejudices and without foundation. There was, however, one curious incident. A Penzance man called at the cottage one day and said confidently: 'There's cannabis growing all along this coast, and I bet there are people within a few miles of here who know what is going on down your cliff.'

My two friends came back to me a few days later with their report, and after they had told me of their experience I quickly put a call through to the CID. 'It would be unwise,' I said, 'to talk over the open line, so could you come out?' And they replied they would be with me on the morrow.

'At one pub,' one of my friends had said, 'we were sitting at a table with two young locals. I wanted a packet of cigarettes and I left the table to go to the bar to buy it. On my return one of the locals said to me: "You're throwing your money away on stuff like that. What you need is a *real* smoke, something you can get a kick out of. I can put you on where you can get it, expensive but it's worth it, and it's available not twenty minutes away from here."'

My friend went on: 'I did not react by showing too much interest. I went on talking about other subjects, then I popped in the question as to where this drug source could be contacted ... but the two locals wavered and said they could only disclose the exact whereabouts of the source if we could prove we were genuinely interested. I am afraid I hedged. I don't mind making enquiries, but neither of us want to get too involved. I did, however, get the names of the two locals.'

The CID officers arrived the next morning, and I reported what my undercover friends had told me.

'What were their names?' was the quick question as soon as I had finished.

I handed over a piece of paper with the names on it.

'That's why I didn't want to tell you this on the open line,' I explained.

We were once again sitting in the porch, no rain dropping on their heads this time, for I had covered the leaking glass roof with polythene. There was, however, an immediate interruption.

I hadn't given the Lager Louts their breakfast, and one of them arrived on the glass roof and forthwith began his blackmailing tactics to attract my attention. I shouted, 'Shut up!'

His method is first to tap gently, then speed the tapping, as if he was trying to imitate Fred Astaire. Then, when I still do not respond, he taps more loudly. Next, when I still do not respond, he stops tapping, and begins ferociously to knock the glass with his beak. His tactics get on my nerves and, as on this occasion, I shouted: 'Shut up!' I get angry because I consider that he is using a form of gull blackmail; and this is especially so when I am sitting indoors on the sofa, quietly reading or writing.

This attitude of mine can, however, result in misunderstandings. There was the occasion when I yelled, 'Shut up' . . . then sensed that it was not the usual sound of a gull knock. I got up and went to the porch. I was just in time to see the back of an elderly lady hastening away.

'I beg your pardon,' I called after her, 'I thought you were a gull!'

'Do you recognize either of these names?' I asked the policemen.

There was no response. Instead they began to question me as to whether I had noticed any suspicious people around at unusual times, and I had to confess that I hadn't.

'What about you?' I asked. 'You must have informers and so on, and I thought you might have picked up something interesting.'

I had a niggling feeling that they might be keeping information from me. I used to have the same feeling when I was in MI5. Nigel West, in his book *A Matter of Trust* (*MI5 1945–1972*), quotes me from my book *The Way to Minack*, giving a description of this feeling:

I have always found it difficult to get down to facts with my MI5 colleagues. There was so much secrecy within secrecy. My colleagues were charming and amiable, conscientious and erudite, but sometimes when I was talking to one of them a glazed expression would come over his face; and I would try to make up my mind whether he was hiding information from me or whether he felt at a disadvantage because I had shown I knew more than he did.

I had also become aware of another aspect to the situation. It had come to me suddenly during one of those three o'clock in the morning wakes which taunt you with overstressed, imaginative worries. One of these had shaken me into thinking that the police, quite possibly, might be pointing at me as the cannabis grower down my cliff. After all, it was I who knew the cliff meadows intimately, and the hidden meadows were within five minutes of the cottage. Could the CID officers, and their distant head office superiors, be treating me as a suspect? The idea enraged me, although it was only the product of a three-o'clock-in-the-morning wake. I was enraged because someone, somewhere, had placed me in this situation.

'What about you?' I asked again.

Cherry had jumped up on the table. Once a timid cat, she had been developing a friendliness, a wish to be noticed, that sometimes irked me. I would, for instance, be in full flow telling a story when Cherry would jump on the table and I would immediately lose the attention of my audience.

'Oh, isn't she pretty! Look at her apricot shirt front . . . listen to her purring!' And then comes the inevitable question: 'How old is she?'

My answer comes out parrot fashion. 'There is no age here,' I say. 'It is a timeless place. The rocks around here are a million years old. Why is society so obsessed by age?'

'We have made wide enquiries,' said one of the officers, 'but we haven't got a lead from them. We have been trying to track the route they take to reach the meadows. We have made enquiries in the Lamorna area, but no one we asked had anything unusual to report. They had to carry things to the meadows from time to time – the wire netting, for instance, the tools to break open the meadows and then, of course, the plants. Quite a job to carry the plants all the way from the Lamorna car park along the cliff path to the meadows, yet the people in the cove near the car park have seen nothing unusual such as a car being parked there late at night.'

'How odd,' I said, thinking again of my three-o'clock-in-the-morning wake.

'And we have checked on the people that live in the lane above the hotel which leads to the coastal path,' went on the officer. 'They have seen nothing. One of them has three dogs, guard dogs he calls them, and whenever someone passes his house at night they bark. He's heard nothing.'

'So how do you think they get there?' I asked boldly.

'Perhaps from the sea,' the man replied.

'Impossible,' I said. 'Except in very calm weather . . . but your remark gives me an idea. It is possible there may be fishermen who are involved in the drug trade who sail along this coast, know it intimately and who pinpointed the isolation of my meadows, knowing that I no longer use them, and passed the information on to someone who was looking for a cannabis-growing site.'

'If they don't come from the sea,' continued the officer, 'and they don't come from Lamorna, they must come from the Land's End direction . . . yet they can't carry their stuff a long way and they must park their car somewhere.'

Again I was reminded of my three-o'clock-in-the-morning wake.

'What happens next?' I asked.

'Well,' said the second officer, 'we're going down to the meadows to see what stage the cannabis plants have reached.'

They got up and left, leaving an outstretched, sound-asleep Cherry on the table.

I reckoned they would be away for an hour. I began to peruse a file in which I had stored my personal papers and diaries during my period in the War Office at the beginning of the Hitler war and which I had unearthed from the Confusion Room the previous night. I had joined up the day before war broke out in the Duke of Cornwall's Light Infantry, and for three months I patrolled Falmouth Docks until someone at the War Office learned I had recently returned from a world tour during which I paid a lightening visit to China. On the basis of this visit I stopped being a private, was promoted to a captain in the Intelligence

118

Corps, posted to the War Office and put in charge of the Chinese Order of Battle. I was also responsible for the Chief of Staff's interpretation of the activities of the Netherlands East Indies Army, the Thai Army and the Indo-Chinese Army. A patrolling private one week, a bewildered Intelligence officer the next.

My period at the War Office, before I was transferred to the secret world of MI5, involved me in two historic occasions. I was the night duty officer when the Germans invaded Norway, the only link between the outside military world and the Chiefs of Staff. I was resting on my iron bedstead when the telephone rang and a reporter from the *Daily Express* asked: 'Does the War Office know the Germans are in Norway?'

I replied, 'No, thanks for the tip.'

Thereupon I contacted a general in bed at home.

'Hitler's invaded Norway, sir.'

A pause.

'What a bloody fool the man is. Act quickly and we've got him.'

I happened to be night duty officer again when the invasion proper began, and this time I heard the news over a crackling line from the Military Attaché in Brussels. Once again I contacted a senior general. 'The balloon is up, sir,' I said.

Came the reply: 'Good . . . now we can get moving.'

I felt sometimes that I was in an Alice in Wonderland world during my time in the War Office. For instance I remember a harassed senior officer garnering information for a statement to be made by Neville

Chamberlain to the House of Commons about Norway. He glared at a meek junior officer who had told him that Narvick had been captured. 'Dammit,' he said, 'you've got the letter wrong. It can't be Narvick, it must be Larvick.' Narvick was in the north, Larvick in the south; and of course Narvick had been captured by surprise. It was several weeks later that a document came my way which I illicitly copied down in my diary. Its date, was 17 May 1940. It came from the Military Secretary of the Chief of Staff:

I think it will be generally agreed that our experience in Scandinavia has shown that we are sadly lacking in topographical information about countries in which we may have to fight. I may be wrong but my impression is that we knew little of port facilities at Andalnes and Namsos, of the roads in the area and of possible landing grounds in northern and central Norway. All our reconnaissance had to be done after operations had begun. We cannot afford to be caught out in the same way in other theatres . . . it may not be too late if we start at once to gather the information we need, and are prepared to spend money to gain it.

There are also in my diary the conclusions of the Chief of Staff's meeting dated 27 May 1940:

I am instructed to draft a report to the War Cabinet drawing attention to the need of a higher state of readiness in the United Kingdom and to the danger of a seaborne raid on a large scale by fast motor boats which the Navy would have difficulty in intercepting and accompanied by airborne raids inland.

Meanwhile on 20 May, exasperated by the lacka-
daisical attitude, the lack of imagination, the lack of
urgency, I wrote the following memorandum to
Colonel Menzies, head of MI6 and a friend of my
father's, outlining a scheme which I believed should be
implemented without delay.

I have no right to bother you with what may well be a ludicrous idea, but I put the idea direct to you because I believe
the urgency of the situation absolves me from putting it
forward through the 'usual channels', and I hope you will
not think it to be just the fantastic product of a layman's
mind. Briefly the idea is this:

1. It is based on the assumption of the invasion of Britain
   by German troops.
2. In this event, agents no doubt will have to be organized to
   operate behind their lines.
3. I suggest that the basis of such an organization should be set
   up immediately in the following way:

   (a) In each area where airborne troops can be
   landed, someone should be appointed who
   knows the locality and local inhabitants intimately and who will act as senior Intelligence
   Officer.
   (b) Under him should be locals who up to the
   present probably have little knowledge of military
   affairs.
   (c) These should be instructed as soon as possible regarding what constitutes information of
   military value.
   (d) Finally the question of the sending out of the

> information should be considered . . . the establish-
> ment of radio transmitting sets etc.

As I have already said these suggestions may be very amateur, but I thought that even if they are, no harm is done by
putting them forward.

Four days later, 24 May, I received a reply. Its lack of
urgency dismayed me.

'I always like new ideas,' wrote Colonel Menzies, 'and
for that reason your letter of the 20th was welcome.
I do not say that what you suggest is practical, but it
will receive consideration *when plans are evolved*.'
[My italics.]

There was a weird outcome. In the second week of
June I learnt that my 'amateur' idea had been put into
action. I learnt this not from Colonel Menzies, but
from my father. He had been appointed to organize
with all speed an intelligence service which would operate behind enemy lines in Somerset, Devon and
Cornwall.

I had also two extracts in my diary from telegrams
sent by Churchill to President Roosevelt; and I remember how moved I was when I read them. The first was
dated 16 June 1940.

We realize fully that the moment Hitler finds he cannot dic-
tate a Nazi peace in Paris he will turn his fury on us. We
shall do our best to withstand it and if we succeed, wide new
doors are opened on the future and all will come out even in
the end.

Derek, who at this time wanted to join the Royal Navy.

On the River Aar, Germany.

The ship bringing coal from Wales, moored in Porth Bay, Newquay, Cornwall.

My mother and father.

Mary the Maltese terrier and
Lance the Old English sheepdog.

In my Strudebaker when a
columnist for the *Daily Mirror*.

Passport photo.

Glendorgal, St Columb Minor.

My mother with Pickle her
Maltese terrier.

Jeannie, Monty, mother and me.

My mother at Minack in our first year.

Jeannie, in our first year.

Digging potatoes.

Jeannie.

Jeannie.

Taken the last time Jeannie and I went out together, for lunch aboard
HMS Cardiff in Falmouth.

Susie and Merlin.

Cherry.

The second was in reply to Roosevelt's reply to the first one:

Your magnificent message ... all the far-reaching plans, strategic, economic, political and moral which your message compounds, may be stillborn if the French cut out now.

All that lonely time when the British were on their own, I made spasmodic notes describing the mood and atmosphere. Here are a few of them.

May 14th ... I have fear chilling my heart. They've broken through at Sedan and there seems nothing to stop them. They're like a steam engine rolling down a field of ants. We have the spirit but what can the spirit do against steel and steel and more steel? Paris looks like being in their hands in a week.

May 20th ... We in the War Office feel pretty grim, but the general public haven't a clue how near we are to total defeat. I feel like getting drunk every night ... I can't stick going home alone ... if only I had a girl to love. There's a Rumanian girl called Leni who is adorable, but she is evacuating to America any time now, and anyhow she's not the girl I'm looking for.

May 26th ... A man from GHQ in France arrived in the office yesterday, and said that the BEF commanders were full of confidence (complacency?). How can they be confident when their soldiers are being driven day by day towards the sea? Oh, what this country suffered from the so-called leaders during the phony war period, their lack of imagination, any sense of urgency, any common sense. Someone in the office said this morning he could list a dozen who ought to be shot. Abbeville has fallen, there's fighting in Boulogne. The BEF are cut off from their supplies, and are about to be surrounded.

June 5th . . . Belgium surrendered and we in the War Office expected that the BEF would be slaughtered and forced to surrender. They had scanty supplies and were in a hopeless strategic position. Yet last Sunday the Empire devoted the day to prayer, and in the ensuing week the miracle took place . . . 335,000 Allied troops were saved . . . spirit had overcome steel. The *New York Times* has celebrated with a magnificent tribute.

> 'As long as the English tongue survives, the word "Dunkirk" will be spoken with reverence. In that harbour, such a hell as never blazed on earth before, at the end of a lost battle, the rags and blemishes that had hidden the soul of democracy, fell away.'

June 10th . . . How moving it is to see in the streets the uniforms of the countries of Europe like the Poles, the Norwegians, Dutch, Czechs and so on, men who have decided to fight on beside us . . . and there is a French general called de Gaulle who has joined us, and who is rallying true Frenchmen to carry on. I had lunch with one of them yesterday, and how ashamed he is of Pétain and his government. The French had pledged that they would never sign a separate peace, but we were ready to release them of this if they did not hand their fleet over to the Germans, but this is what they are doing. And they have even handed over 400 Nazi airmen who were to be transferred to British prisoner of war camps. But now these skilled men will bomb us.

June 23rd . . . Fighting for democracy sounds such a nice phrase. Yet I sometimes wonder whether it is not just a smug phrase, for there is so much wrong with democracy. It has needed Churchill to try and cut away the rot in it. Its tortoise speed methods have brought us to the present disastrous situation. We take so long to make up our minds to do anything. Committees proliferate and decisions are fudged. I see examples every day here at the War Office. Snap decisions which are so necessary to meet the immediate crisis are delayed. Individuals who press a point are despised. Fresh ideas are not considered. Plans progress at tortoise speed. We need action. Thank God Churchill is now Prime Minister, but oh what a job he's got to get rid of the old guard.

July 7th . . . Four days ago I had my two bottom wisdom teeth taken out, and after two days in the nursing home, I've continued my discomfort in mother's flat. She is ideal. She does everything possible for me yet hasn't that persistent kindness of some unselfish people. For instance when she rang me at the nursing home and suggested me convalescing with her, I at first pooh-poohed the idea. She said no more, she didn't press it. She let the idea sink into me so that I was able to come to my own conclusion to realize it was a wonderful ideal.

July 20th . . . We are living on the edge of a precipice, invasion might come at any moment, but you wouldn't think so if you saw the people going about their work. They believe themselves invincible, and Hitler will never come. They are still far away from the real horrors of war. I was with a young Canadian today, perhaps twenty years old, who had fought in France. His words crushed me. 'He was lying with his throat half cut away, with half an hour to live, begging us to shoot him . . . but none of us dared. We left him behind to meet the Boche alone.'

August 4th . . . Twenty-six years ago today World War I began. How is it possible that world leaders could let it happen again?

September 5th . . . Hitler's softening up of Britain has begun. Bombs are nightly raining on London. We have arrived at the reality of civilian war.

Here are snippets, odds and ends reflecting the times:

'We'll muddle through . . . we always win the last battle.'

'Speaking of unpleasant facts is defeatism . . . of pleasant facts wishful thinking.'

Gone with the Wind at three cinemas in London.

Silver-coloured barrage balloons in the sky.

The song: 'It's a lovely day tomorrow'.

The rage for striptease in nightclubs and the rage against it.

'The less one thinks these days, the better for one's peace of mind.'

Chocolate is a rarity.

Union Jacks are flown on battered, bombed houses.

Air-raid workers wear white tin hats with the initial of their particular function on them.

The Forces requisition houses at forty-eight hours' notice.

The meat ration is 1/3d worth a week. Butter an ounce a week, bacon four ounces. No silk stockings available. You can buy one razor blade a week. A 12 hp car is allowed six gallons of petrol a month. Eggs are rare. There is no cheese to be had.

'I was in the last show, you know.'

'All the things you are.'

'There will always be an England.'

A man said to me the other day after France had surrendered, with a smile, 'Well, we've got through to the final.'

'Begin is the Beguine.'

Tea is rationed to two ounces a week.

I left the War Office and my Chinese Order of Battle in September, went on an Intelligence course and was then transferred to MI5. In January I was given the assignment of covering the press world. It was a very wide assignment, and I was given much freedom to create my own circle of contacts. Once a week I had a meeting with the heads of MI5 departments at which I reported the mood of the press world, and also inside stories which were not getting into print. It was a practical job in other ways. Many of the stories I recounted would often be used by the Double Cross section, passing them on to the German Abwehr as if they were coming from a German spy in London.

On 12 January my book *Time was Mine* was published. It had a warm welcome but a fortnight after publication it suffered a disaster. During a night of heavy bombing on the City, a landmine fell on Paternoster Row near St Paul's where my books were stored before being sent out to bookshops. It was devastating. Many copies had already been distributed, however, and I had a wonderful review by Hannen Swaffer, most cynical and most powerful of columnists, and I had splendid compliments from Negley Farson, author of *The Way of a Transgressor*, whom I had long hero-worshipped. And there was another bonus.

At Christmas I had spent three days at my Cornish home of Glendorgal, a place I loved so much that when I was at Harrow I chose to go there instead of the fashionable Eton and Harrow match at Lord's. At Christmas it was wild, blustery weather with sudden outbursts of thundery rain, but this did not worry me. I was released from the London stress. I wandered along the cliffs and walked barefoot on Porth Beach. I crossed the stream to Porth Island where my mother was to donate a granite seat in memory of my father who worshipped Glendorgal. I roamed around, strolled several times to the point, sat in the little stone shelter and I pondered there. I pondered about the girl I wanted to find, a girl who would give me a steadiness against the restless, threatening background of my life, a girl who would love the same things as I did, who would effortlessly join me in the happiness of walking barefoot on Porth Beach, wandering along the cliffs undaunted by blustery outbursts of rain, a girl who would intuitively become a part of my life. Just a dream. I felt no girl could fulfil that dream. Meanwhile I was alone.

I returned to London, to the bombs and to the excitement of *Time was Mine* being published, and the miracle took place. The day after publication I was in the Savoy with a friend, standing by the reception desk, when my friend, a newspaperman with an opportunist outlook said, 'Do you see that very pretty girl standing by the hall porter?'

'Yes,' I replied, having noticed her already.

'Well,' my friend said, 'you ought to meet her. Her name is Jean Nicol, and she is in charge of publicity for the Savoy Hotel Group. If you are nice to her she might put your book on the Savoy bookstall.'

Needless to say I *was* nice to her. I gave her a copy and a week later she said she had loved it, and flattered me by saying she couldn't put it down . . . and she put it on the bookstall. I thanked her and asked her out to dinner.

The Minack Chronicles story had begun.

The CID officers ought to be back any time now. The nineteenth-century clock which stands on the chest in the sitting room struck one o'clock. It is a gentle sound, not one which one would think would startle people, but it does. I am sitting with visitors in the porch, then comes the striking note of the clock.

People's reactions are curious. Men, for instance, react like cowboys in a Western movie. A hand will dash to a back pocket where a revolver is kept at the ready. Women hear the gentle announcement of the time, momentarily freeze, and then look as if a gorilla had entered their bedroom . . . and all the while it is the sound of the clock which the directors of the Savoy Hotel had given Jeannie when she left the company to come to Minack.

There is another clock hanging on the wall in the kitchen, a clock which makes me feel sad sometimes in view of it story. I bought it, having traced it with some difficulty, from a chandler in the docklands of London. It is a ship's clock. Jeannie had told me, that first Christmas we had together after we had married, that she longed to have a ship's clock, and so I gave her this clock that Christmas.

Then on 20 February, while we were celebrating our first wedding anniversary, a bomb fell on our house. The clock, round and garnished with brass, had been a central feature of the sitting room. It had been placed above the fireplace and become very much a part of our newly married life. The bomb created chaos in the sitting room, but after we had recovered from the shock we found, amid the chaos, the ship's clock was still ticking.

It thereupon became a symbol for us in that it made us believe that so long as the clock ticked our lives would run smoothly. An absurd notion, perhaps, but much of the orchestra of life relies on absurd notions to keep us in balance against the logical demands of today.

It ticked all through Jeannie's lifetime, and then it stopped. For a while I took no steps to repair it because I did not want it to leave Minack and be lodged on some workshop bench where the repairer would have no knowledge of its history. But I had luck. I was told of a clock mender called Finch whose premises were near Falmouth and I asked him to call. I found he was on the same wavelength as myself, and that he understood my feelings for this silent ship's clock.

I heard voices, then around the corner by the water butt came the two CID officers.

'How did you get on?' I asked, and both of them smiled.

'Lovely down there,' one of them said. 'A different world. Lovely and quiet up here but down there in those cliff meadows . . .'

'You see, then,' I said, 'why it tears my heart that someone betrayed me by growing the cannabis.'

'Easy to understand,' he said. Then he added: 'They are the best cannabis plants we have ever seen!'

IX

I had a birthday party for Merlin in early April. There have been donkey birthday parties before. Fred, for instance, of *A Donkey in the Meadow* had such a gala of a birthday party that it was filmed by the BBC, a hilarious occasion when the children of the local school of St Buryan were his guests. The film has been repeated several times on BBC2. Merlin's party, however, was a very intimate affair. No cascade of laughing children. No Mr Miller playing his barrel organ. No specially made birthday cake. No ice cream smudging his nostrils.

The party was held in the big field of Oliver land, close to the gate which has at its side Jeannie's sign A PLACE FOR SOLITUDE, the sign that Jeannie kissed. I had brought with me a variety of foods which would appeal to the guests. I had pony pellets, packets of Rich Tea biscuits, carrots, apples, packets of sunflower seeds, a mixture of corn and barley, and peanuts. The guests all belonged to the local population. There were Merlin and Susie, the robin who lives in the wild land nearby but who mysteriously disappears around May time for the rest of the summer, Charlie chaffinch and his mate who regularly haunt the porch, Rupert the pheasant, and the two Lager Louts who, typically, gatecrashed.

132

There was also Cherry. She accompanied me up the lane then, when I climbed over the gate into the field, she sensibly became an observer, sitting on the gravel watching.

It was a beautiful setting. I sat on a rock near Jeannie's Shelter, looking at the celandines brimming the field, the green of meadows folding into the quiet sea of Mount's Bay, the air full of the growing scents of spring, the white of a sailing ship of a cloud billowing against the blue sky . . . I sat there while Merlin's guests waited impatiently for the party to begin. I struggled to prise open the wrapper of a Rich Tea biscuit packet, Merlin and Susie pushing their noses at me.

Packet open! And I gave a layer of biscuits to Merlin, a layer to Susie. Crunch, crunch, crunch! The Lager Louts, potty for such biscuits, were strutting on the grass a few yards away, waggling their tail feathers, watching me hopefully, greedily, and I tossed them each a biscuit. They scurried to collect them, instantly breaking them with their beaks and swallowing them, then asking for more. The robin was on top of the stone post behind me and he too wanted a Rich Tea biscuit, but it had to be broken so he was able to peck at the crumbs.

There is a strange connection between a robin and Jeannie. The morning that Jeannie died I went to see my friends John Miller, the famous painter, and Michael Truscott, the well-known potter and picture restorer at Sancreed where they lived. After saying a normal goodbye I got into the car ready to leave, but stayed on for several minutes talking to John. Then I finally said goodbye and set off. A minute later I was startled by a chirruping, and there on my shoulder was a robin. I stopped the car, said a few words of endearment to the robin, because I was naturally in need of endearment myself, then opened the window and the robin flew up into a tree where it sat warbling a song. I was very moved. A few days later my friend David Cornwell was preparing the superb tribute he was to give about Jeannie at her service, when he left his desk to have a walk along the cliffs. When he returned a robin was sitting on the manuscript he had been writing. He had never seen a robin in his house before. And so this robin who lived by the solitude gate made me want to call it Jeannie. I have never done so, but the temptation is there.

Meanwhile the greedy festivities continued. Charlie the chaffinch and his mate gorged themselves on the corn and barley, while Rupert had a handful of peanuts to himself. For Merlin and Susie there were second and third courses – fresh carrots followed by apples cut in half. Then they spied I was holding another packet of Rich Tea biscuits, so Merlin pushed his nose at me again. Once more I struggled to open it, tearing at the wrapper which seemed designed to prevent anyone opening it like other packets of the same type, but when I succeeded the donkeys were delighted, and within seconds there were the munch, munch sounds of contentment.

'From now on,' I warned them, 'you both will be on a diet.'

Charlie the chaffinch and his mate wanted more corn and barley, which I provided, and Rupert wanted yet more peanuts. I threw another handful into the grass where he picked at it a few feet away from the donkeys who were accustomed to his presence. Rupert was always on his own. He was a vulnerable pheasant, if one can call a pheasant vulnerable. Rupert, I believe, was an offspring of the General, the cock pheasant who, before he died, reigned in the Minack area, a harem of lady pheasants in his wake. Not so Rupert. I have never seem him with a lady pheasant. He roams Oliver land and appears to be content, but there is little doubt that he looks to me for extra supplies of food. He will be waiting at the solitude gate when I go there to feed the donkeys in late afternoon; and if the donkeys are not there but down by the stable gate near the cottage, I will see him making the journey down the land to the porch door. Often I do not see him coming, but he has a way of gaining my attention. He thumps the porch door with his bottom.

He runs a risk, however, by coming to the cottage for a cock pheasant has appropriated the area. He is called Hullabaloo, so named because of his frequent loud cries with which he shatters the quiet countryside. He is no General with a harem, but he has a very forceful character and I am afraid there would be a bitter fight if he and Rupert met on Minack territory. He has this spring a small lady pheasant as a companion who will be having a nest somewhere in the meadows and whom Hullabaloo will protect from predators. The other day he also protected Cherry.

A bully cat, a ferocious dark brown tom, sometimes appears around the cottage. I am scared of him because bullying toms will sometimes attack and kill a neutered female, and one day I saw this nearly happen. I heard cat screams outside, and a minute later Cherry came hurtling into the cottage followed by the bully cat who almost caught her as she raced into the sitting room and under my desk. Cherry, kitten-sized Cherry, would have had no chance had bully cat caught her. On another occasion this could have happened had it not been for Hullabaloo. He had been making his usual noises outside my bedroom window when suddenly he changed them into a cluck-cluck. It was an alarm note. I went to the window and there was the bully cat stalking Cherry. At the same instant Cherry saw him and began her race to safety. It became my turn to do the scaring . . . the bully cat fled.

The party was over, but I continued to sit on the rock. Merlin and Susie had wandered off into the middle of the field, the chaffinches and the robin had disappeared, the Lager Louts had flown off towards Carn Barges and the sea. Rupert was slowly making his way along the M walk, the walk that M took when she carried Ambrose in his little basket to the honeysuckle meadow. I sat there wondering, natural peace around me.

I wondered why full employment is considered a pos-sibility when the computer, in the name of efficiency, is draining jobs away. I wondered what was to happen to those who have done their training at universities and who find there are no jobs for them to go to. I sensed their feelings of hopelessness for they find, like others who have been made redundant, that they have lost a motivation in life. I wondered why the silent majority is allowing freedom to be chiselled away. How is it that the kill-joys have so much power as to destroy the freedoms of centuries? No one is allowed to flirt be-cause the kill-joys call it sexual harassment. No one is allowed to show harmless affection for a child without the threat of being charged with child abuse. Violent crime is condoned by ignoring the adage of letting the 'punishment fit the crime'.

That attitude would be justified if violent crime had not proliferated. Two generations ago recalcitrant chil-dren were punished with a slipper or a cane, and they grew up respecting the law. There were no mindless gangs roaming the streets. The mindless gangs, and the violent criminals, came when the do-gooders decided that discipline was antisocial, and that a prison should be as comfortable as a holiday camp. Surely it would be more progressive to outline the horrible conditions of prison so that a criminal would think twice about risking the chance of being sent there. And there is another way, it seems to me, which would help to reduce crime. Why is there not a media campaign against receivers of stolen goods, including those people in society who buy stolen goods? Smash the receivers, and you smash the suppliers.

Then my mind roamed around a current exposure in a newspaper of the private life of an Air Marshall with vivid descriptions by a former girlfriend. The Air Marshall had an invincible record of service to the country, the girl had no such record. None the less the Air Marshall had to resign as the result of the girl's revelations in the newspaper. Thus a brilliant mind was lost to the RAF. Similar situations are taking place regularly in all walks of life, and such incidents make me contemplate the effect on history had the media and the kill-joys been in power in past times.

There would have been no Trafalgar, for instance. Nelson would no longer have been in the Royal Navy because he would have been forced to resign owing to his association with Emma Hamilton. There would have been no Waterloo because the Duke of Wellington would have been hounded out of the Army due to his association with Harriet Wilson. Lloyd George would never have become Prime Minister ... all through the years men and women have received inspiration from a love affair, achieving greatness as a result. But now many public persons of talent are so harassed by the media and the kill-joys that they choose not to seek a public role.

'We know no spectacle' wrote Macaulay 'so ridiculous as the British public in one of its periodical fits of morality.'

I had forgotten Cherry. I had forgotten she had

stayed in the lane while the party was in progress, and now suddenly she was at my feet. 'Cherry,' I said, bending down to stroke the top of her little black head, 'this is just the moment I needed you.' And she opened her little mouth, displayed a rim of white teeth and gave me a silent miaow.

I needed her because my roaming thoughts had strayed from public affairs to my own affairs. I had a sudden feeling that Jeannie was with me listening to my thoughts, and the feeling choked me.

It is the same for most of us who have suffered loss. We appear cheerful, we feel cheerful, and then suddenly an emotional dagger pierces us. There is no time limit in the coming of that dagger. It will strike at an elderly woman who long ago, when in her teens, said goodbye to a young man on a station platform who was going off to the Front and whom she never saw again.

I sat there thinking about what I missed about Jeannie besides her beauty, dark hair falling to her shoulders, her sylph-like figure, her voice. When I first met her, and we were speaking to each other on the telephone, I used to ask her to go on talking, saying anything, just so I could listen to her voice. I miss her sophisticated innocence, her ability to deal with any occasion yet appear so natural. I have seen her so many times at the Savoy, at Claridge's at the Berkeley, reigning as hostess at a luncheon or a party, looking delicious and almost child-like, and her guests would be famous names from all over the world. I miss her fun, her enthusiasms, her interest in politics, in tennis, cricket, football and every aspect of general news. There was endless conversation between us; and when she was with other people she stimulated them because she could speak with knowledge of their own interests. An Oxford don who knew Jeannie said of her, quoting St Simon's description of a French contemporary: 'She gave wit to those who had none.'

I miss her subtle practical help. She would care for me when I was writing the Minack books, sending me off into my cabin in the wood or down to the bottom of the cliff, saying that she would look after everything and everyone who might come to interrupt my day. I did, as I have said, the same for her when she was writing *Meet Me at the Savoy* by locking her in the spare room and saying I wouldn't let her out until she had written four pages. She was kinder to me. After a day's work, as dusk was falling I would walk out of the cottage, and thread my way through the undergrowth to the cabin in the wood. It was lit by calor gas and there was a small calor gas heater. I would sit there at my typewriter free of outside interference amid silence and growing darkness. I would sit there stumbling my words out, thankful it was no word processor so when I read a page which I considered to be rubbish I was able to get rid of my frustration by tearing the offending page out of the typewriter and throwing it into the wastepaper basket. Then Jeannie would appear through the darkness, a torch shining, with a glass of whisky to restore my morale. And I would cry out:

'Darling, how did you guess? How did you know that I needed this whisky so badly?' Jeannie had carried the glass in the darkness through to me. The last time she did this was when I was writing *The Cherry Tree*, the story of Cherry's arrival at Minack. Now Cherry was purring on my lap, and in the cabin the wastepaper basket is still full of crumpled pages that I had torn out of my typewriter. I have never written in the cabin since *The Cherry Tree*. It was the last book for which Jeannie typed the fair copy.

I miss her everyday running of the cottage. I miss her help in solving my problems. I miss the restraint she had on me when I displayed over-excitement about some incident which had upset me. I miss her caring for the birds and animals. I miss her moments of wildness. I miss the way she could cope with difficult situations, often turning them into fun situations. There was, the occasion, for instance, when George Brown the lovable controversial Labour politician resigned from being Foreign Secretary in Harold Wilson's government, then invited himself and his wife Sophie to come to Minack to get away from the press and find peace. His tantrums, his sometimes appalling behaviour, his drinking habits, his immense charm, and his brilliant mind had become legendary in the sixties and seventies.

George Brown [wrote his biographer, Pater Paterson] made more of a mark in the public imagination than any other member of the two Labour Governments he served. He was accident prone, outspoken to an extent rare among modern politicians, intensely patriotic, hard working, even harder drinking, tyrannical towards his subordinates, quick as a Gascon to take offence in any company . . . and as swift to apologize for any offence given.

Above all George Brown's most enduring monument is that more stories, both true and apocryphal, were told of him than of any other politician since Churchill. The result was to make him more popular with the British public, of all political persuasions, than any other Labour politician in the history of the Party. This could fairly be said of George Brown that, for all his faults, as was said of Palmerston: 'He loved his country, and his country loved him.'

The onset of their stay was not auspicious. They were due to arrive in time for dinner. Jeannie was cooking a roast chicken, and this was to be followed by strawberries and cream. We had a variety of drinks at hand out of politeness, although our past experiences in George's company had never featured his alcohol reputation. A sherry or two, and that was all. It was as if he only let himself go with the strain of being under public scrutiny. Anyhow there we were, Jeannie and I, ready for the occasion and dinner time came and went and there was no George and Sophie.

Nine o'clock, ten o'clock, eleven o'clock, and still no George and Sophie. We kept walking up the slope above the cottage, positioning ourselves beside the galvanized tin on the top of the well where we could see the smeared lights of a car turning off the main road and starting up the lane towards the farm buildings, then on down the hill to Minack, down the lane which got narrower and narrower as it reached Monty's Leap and the cottage beyond. We stood there peering into the darkness. Midnight . . . still no smear of a car's head-lights, and then suddenly . . .

'They are on the way!' I called out.

We watched the smear coming swiftly towards the farm buildings, then momentarily clear of the hedges guarding the lane, the smear turned into headlights then back into a smear again as the car made its down-ward journey along the Minack lane.

'He's travelling very fast,' I said nervously.

The car had now reached the turn at the far side of Monty's Leap. There was no slackening in its speed. We had run down the path to the space beside the stable where all cars had to stop. Jeannie was ahead of me.

The car had leapt Monty's Leap and was heading for both of us.

'*Stop*, George!' Jeannie shouted.

It wasn't George.

It was a police car.

George had had a collision at the Exeter roundabout. He had asked the police to let us know that he would not be arriving until the next day.

After that we had a quiet time. For five days we did not move away from Minack. Jeannie effortlessly pre-pared the meals in the galley of a kitchen and was the same unselfconscious hostess as she would have been at Claridge's. George flirted with her, Sophie gossiped.

'All these terrible situations George gets himself into . . . George has such remorse in the morning!'

'So important, Jeannie, to have nice shoes. There I am sitting on a platform, George making his speech, and I have the feeling those at the meeting are looking at my shoes.'

'What do you miss most,' asked Jeannie, 'now that George is out of office?'

'The chauffeur-driven car! How I miss that!'

George, meanwhile, meandered around the land letting time slip by. We talked about politics, about his relationship with Harold Wilson, but he was not wanting the conversation to be deep. He showed no desire for alcohol except for the normal social drink. He was no alcoholic, no secret drinker. It was just that he was highly strung and, like others, he misguidedly would drink (and sherry was his favourite) to reduce his tension. Jeannie and I began their visit in apprehension, but that disappeared on the second day when it was clear that George had relaxed.

We had surrendered the cottage to them, making our sleeping quarters in the Confusion Room. On the second morning I waited till eleven o'clock before going up to the cottage . . . and as I walked up the path I heard a strange bellowing coming from the direction of the small front garden. I turned the corner by the water butt, and found George on this lovely summer morning in an open-neck shirt singing in a rich baritone Puccini's 'Your Tiny Hand is Frozen' from *La Bohème*, while a bewildered donkey, Fred, looked down on him from the field above the garden, playing his part with a crescendo of hee-haws.

The people who visit are on my wavelength, otherwise they would not trouble to come, for Minack is difficult to find. My visitors keep me in touch with the outside world. They belong to every walk of life, and they will belong to different parts of the world. We sit in the porch and have a grass-roots conversation. I waste no time with pleasantries. Within a few minutes I have asked two direct questions – Where do you live? What do you do? – and that will set off a line of conversation that reflects the mood of the times. There will be comments like these:

'I was in Telecom but I've been made redundant. I'm only forty-two, but what happens now? Nobody seems to want a forty-year-old. I thought I was in a job for life, but now I have no motivation.'

'The first industrial revolution created jobs . . . this second industrial revolution is destroying jobs.'

'How can there be full employment when a computer can do the work of thousands?'

'The next five years will see the undeveloped countries becoming the mass producers. Port Sunlight, once the main producer of soap products, is dying. The manufacturing is being transferred to the Far East.'

'Universities and colleges are turning out undergraduates like myself but where are the jobs? I am twenty-three and have all the right qualifications, but the only job I've found is as a temporary waitress.'

145

'Company's accounts should by law have to include a yearly valuation of the emotional cost to employees as a result of making them redundant.'

'I am a mother who wants to bring up her children properly. I found my seven-year-old son taking ice cream from the refrigerator without my permission. I ticked him off verbally and what does he say. He shouts at me that if I tick him off like that again, he will ring up Child Line.'

'I am a teacher, but I can no longer show affection to my pupils. I can never let myself be alone with a child.'

'My little girl said she wanted to cuddle up in my bed. What should I do? The thought went through me that I might be accused of child abuse if I let her.'

' "Suffer the little children to come unto me" has become a dirty phrase.'

'No one can now show a natural affection for a child. Everyone has to be on guard including uncles and other relations. We are all now terrorized by highly organized minority pressure groups. This is not democracy.'

'What rubbish the way newspaper editors declare that they are the guardians of free speech as an excuse for their stories. They are only interested in the circulation of their newspapers.'

'The Royal Family is not a family as such. They represent our history, cultural, political, military, and when we wave our flags we are reflecting that history, and remembering all those who lived and died for that history . . . and many of us are thinking of those of our own families who played their part in it.'

146

'Did you see the two-hour TV programme on Prince Charles? I thought it marvellous to see a man speak with absolute honesty. Such a contrast to the media people who criticize him.'

'To have everyday freedom, there has always been a price to pay. There have to be victims. We can't all win. I am prepared to be a possible victim rather than succumb to the ever-increasing laws which are destroying that freedom.'

'I never understand how the public and the media clamour for tax cuts but at the same time condemn lack of investment in government projects. Why do they think that money comes from the sky?'

People will come just at the moment I need them. For instance the kitchen sink was blocked.

'What do you do?' I asked the visitor who had just sat down in the porch.

'I am a plumber,' he had replied.

'Just the person I need!' I said . . . and the visitor, instead of talking about books, set to work.

A distinguished lawyer called at the cottage at a time when I was beset by a ticklish legal problem. What happens? I disclose my predicament, and for an hour I receive free what normally would have cost a high price. Then there was the occasion when I had returned to Minack with a number of tomato plants for the greenhouse. I was not looking forward to planting them on my own, but when I arrived back there were already two visitors waiting for me.

'What do you do?' I soon asked.

'We are market gardeners,' they said.

And the couple proceeded to plant my tomatoes.

There was the Scotland Yard detective who brought me one of my books to autograph, lending me a pen to do so. As I was signing he distracted my attention by talking about the dangers of adding any special item of value to one's current insurance policy. 'Insurance policies,' he said, 'were once hidden away in files. Today if someone adds an item of value to the policy, it is flashed on a screen. Anyone can see it. It may be a coincidence, but it is odd how often the particular householder concerned has his house robbed.'

I completed my signing and handed him the book. There was a silent moment. 'Excuse me,' said the detective. 'I've seen what you have done!'

I had put his pen in my pocket.

There was the help I received from two friends who have been regular visitors to Minack over several years. They have come regularly in September, staying at Mousehole, and it has been a tradition, from Jeannie days, for them to lunch at Minack on the Tuesday after their arrival from Aberdeen. The menu is always the same: fresh crab and chocolate mousse. Their names are Ken and Arunda Peters. Ken is one of the most distinguished Scotsmen of our time. He was the legendary editor of the *Aberdeen Journal* with its famous high standards of integrity. He followed this with distinguished public appointments ... but it was the *Aberdeen Journal* that brought us together. Long before we were to meet them both, Jeannie's book *Meet Me at the Savoy*, had caught his attention and he had secured second serial rights for his newspaper. Jeannie and I knew nothing about him until one afternoon we saw a couple of figures scrambling over the wall by the stables. I approached them politely, saying, 'Can I help you?' And then ensued the conversation, the disclosure, that this was the man who had helped us at a time of financial crisis.

Here we were having our Tuesday lunch again, and I was telling them of my annoyance at the disappearance of a twenty-foot aluminium pipe. I had looked everywhere for it, and I explained that I could find no sign of it. I added that I was touchy about its disappearance because I vaguely worried that it might have something to do with the cannabis mystery.

I had fixed the pipe across an inlet into an acre of moorland alongside the winding lane. The object of the inlet was to provide a space for a car to back into, should it meet another coming in the opposite direction. The object of the pipe was to stop any parking in the space. The moorland is called Jill's Moor, and the reason is this.

A farmer, two years or so before, had taken over the moorland for the use of his over-wintering steers, prior to sending them to market in the spring. The steers created chaos in the moorland, devouring it bare of underground. The lane to the cottage was also churned into a mud bath by the daily use of the tractor which brought extra fodder to the steers. Something had to be done about it, and it was Jill, a long time reader of the Chronicles, who took action. She asked a friend who owned an aircraft to fly over Minack, and take photographs of the moorland. Jill went with him. My Vodophone rang one afternoon, and it was Jill: 'We're flying above you! Quick, and you'll see us!' The photographs were vivid. The damage to the moorland was enormous . . . and the result of Jill's mission was that the farmer was asked by his landlord to remove the steers. Hence the name of Jill's Moor. It is a beautiful, untamed moorland once again.

A couple of days after the lunch I had a letter from Ken and Arunda. This is what it said (with apologies to Sherlock Holmes and Dr Watson):

After an idyllic day at Minack, we bid farewell to our host and began walking up the winding lane. Mr Holmes's keen and watchful eyes searching the hedgerows and lush vegetation, all very green and wet after the deluging rain which had fallen for a long time that day.

It did not take long for my Baker Street colleague to solve the problem of the missing pipe, the disappearance of which was concerning our host so much. Suddenly Holmes's pace quickened, he gripped my arm intently.

'Look, Watson!' he exclaimed.

There, concealed in the grass verge under a hedgerow of the lane was the missing pipe, about twenty-five yards north of the small clearing which it should have been guarding. There was no doubting our booty. There was the pipe. Who had put it there?

As soon as I had read the letter I went up the lane to retrieve the pipe. There was no sign of it. Had Sherlock Holmes blundered? I could not believe this to be so. I contacted him, and asked him to return and reopen his investigation. My friends returned. They arrived at the cottage in triumph. Between them they were carrying the pipe.

Visitors sometimes buy books. If they hesitate I say cheerfully: 'The cost of a Minack book, specially signed, is the same as a lunch at a restaurant. The lunch lasts two hours, the book lasts a lifetime, and is also a memento of a holiday.' I am inclined, depending on my mood, to be cagey of signing secondhand books, though a book bought at a bookshop I of course will sign. The trouble is that it seems difficult for some people to understand that authors have to survive like everyone else. They are not an offshoot of the social services. It is funny but discouraging whcn, as happened the other day after I had spent an hour talking to a couple, they handed me a worn copy of one of my books, asking me to sign it, saying, 'We bought it at a car boot sale. Such a bargain!'

Visitors often bring presents, generous and thoughtful presents. The donkeys, of course, receive their share, and so does Cherry. Merlin and Susie are given so much that by the end of the summer they should be on a diet. Some of the presents are startling in their generosity. There was, for instance, the American couple from Texas, who arrived with a charming couple from the Midlands.

They had been here before, and I had kept in touch with them. On this occasion they spent much of the day at Minack wandering around, relaxing and sitting in the porch. We had been sitting there for a while when I commented how much I admired the husband's very special Texan belt.

'I've always wanted one like that,' I remarked innocently.

'Have it,' he said, undoing the belt from his trousers and handing it to me.

A couple of hours later we were still in the porch talking, and I had opened a bottle of wine.

Suddenly I said, and there was no ulterior motive in my doing so; indeed I could not believe the sound of my voice as I spoke: 'The material of those blue trousers you are wearing . . . what is it made of? I can't find anything like it in this country.'

'You like them?' asked my Texan friend. 'You can have them!'

He was saved the embarrassment of taking them off. His wife came to the rescue.

'There is a spare pair in the car. I'll fetch them.'

There have been other kinds of visits which I will remember.

I will remember the fifteen-year-old girl who lived in Manchester and who suffered from an acute form of anorexia. She had said to her parents that she desperately wanted to go to Minack because she had a feeling a visit would help her. Her parents had immediately granted her wish. They did not seek difficulties about suddenly driving here. Within twenty-four hours they and the girl had arrived. I was combing Cherry in the porch when I saw her running round the corner of the cottage, thin-faced, emaciated, but ablaze with excitement.

After her visit her specialist sent her to a London hospital for treatment. Her father wrote to me that she had taken several of the Minack Chronicles with her and they were beside her bed. 'The fact they are there,' wrote the father, 'gives her great comfort.'

The treatment was a severe one, and there were times when she despaired. As the months went by she had hopeful times, then setbacks. Occasionally I would get messages from her. One August day a young couple from Bristol called here, and the girl told me she was a professional healer. We were sitting in the porch talking about her work when the telephone rang, and it was, to my surprise, the fifteen-year-old girl (I presumed her father had given her my Vodophone number). I chatted to her. She sounded very normal, and it made me happy that she felt she could ring me. The coincidence in timing though, was extraordinary. Here I was with a professional healer, and the girl had contacted me! I told the healer the full story. She took down the details, and said she would put the girl on her remote healing list.

Meanwhile treatment, requiring much self-discipline and courage on the part of both the girl and her parents, continued; they told me later how inspired they were by the care and patience of the staff of the Atkinson Memorial Hospital in London.

Several months passed. Then, a fortnight ago, what seemed like a miracle took place.

Around the corner of the cottage, the same corner where I had seen a thin-faced, emaciated girl running towards me, came a beautiful young girl, soft hair touching her shoulders, lovely figure, mischievous eyes, and with so much to tell me.

My ruminative period was now over. Merlin and Susie were coming towards me, hoping to find more in the party's larder. Cherry saw them and jumped off my lap, bouncing her way through the grass to the solitude gate.

'No more, no more,' I said to the donkeys.

At that moment I heard the hum of an aircraft, and I could tell that it was flying low, hugging the coastline from the Penzance direction. Nearer, nearer . . . then I saw the top of it skimming along towards Land's End. What was it doing?

I had a hunch what this aircraft, a helicopter, was up to.

I had to wait until after lunchtime the next day to prove that my hunch was correct.

X

The CID officers arrived in the early afternoon of the following day.

I had spent the morning in the Confusion Room, and I was in some state of confusion myself. What should I search through next? Letters I wrote to my family, and they to me during my journey round the world? My diaries? Search for my favourites among the massive collection of records and books? What about the photographs? And there were four suitcases on the top shelf above Labour Warms . . . what was in them?

I felt much curiosity in my task, and was having much pleasure in performing it, but I was missing the support of someone who could help me, someone who would share my enthusiasm, someone who would give me a push when my interest temporarily waned. Jeannie was an expert in such matters, but I could not rely for ever on the memory of Jeannie. I needed tangible help, I had such help in the cottage for two or three hours a week. First, and for several years, there had been Joan, but she had to give up because she became the victim of a bad back. Now I have Tracey who has four young children, but who looks too young to be the mother of four children. Thus I have been lucky. First Joan, now Tracey, and both of them had the special advantage of being on the same wavelength as myself. I have always felt at ease with each of them.

But the tangible help I was seeking was of a different kind. I was seeking inspiration, someone whose presence would light up the crevices in my mind, alerting me to new ideas and challenging me in conversation. It would be misleading if I did not admit that I had visits which fulfilled my desires, but they were temporary visits.

I could not, however, have it both ways. I am not wanting a permanent companion. I want to live my life on my own yet, as single people well know, there are moments when one yearns for a special companion who measures up to what such a companion could be. I had such a companion once when I was writing a book. It was bliss. I was able to ring her up whenever I felt down or, for that matter, whenever I felt elated, and I knew her reactions would always spur me on. She never failed. But that was a temporary situation, and I knew this from the beginning. Even so it remains a situation which I long to repeat. Meanwhile I never feel lonely. I recall the words of Canon Andrews of Stoke Climsland, close friend of Edward, Prince of Wales and that era of the Royal Family including the Queen Mother. He said to me on his hundredth birthday (when he was still living on his own): 'The best thing about living on one's own is being able to make a bloody fool of yourself, and nobody knows!'

The CID officers, the same couple as before, sat down in the porch and one of them produced a large envelope and laid it on the table.

156

'Did you see a helicopter flying low along the coast yesterday?' he asked.

'Yes,' I said.

'The two of us were in it. It was the police helicopter and we were taking photographs along the coastline, not just photographs of your meadow, but checking whether there were any other sites being used.'

'I had guessed it might be something like that.'

He opened the envelope and handed me the photographs. They were very clear prints and they showed very clearly the four meadows, the four Minack meadows which were being used; and they showed the extent of the undergrowth which surrounded them, like a clearing within a jungle.

'You can see now,' continued the officer, 'that only someone who knew this area intimately would ever have known the meadows existed.'

'Among them fishermen,' I said, 'who sail close along the coast all through the year.'

'What do you mean?'

'I've mentioned it before to you. A fisherman could have observed that I was no longer working the meadows, and passed the information on to a cannabis grower looking for a site.'

'Do you personally know any fishermen?'

'I don't know any. I only know what people say about some of them. A happy-go-lucky lot. Nothing sinister.'

Jeannie and I, soon after we had first arrived, made friends of a fisherman called Ned Tregenza who

157

moored his boat at Mousehole. We were in the Ship at Mousehole one evening, and over the drinks we got talking about fishing nets with Ned. We explained that we had this notion of becoming independent of most food supplies. We would grow all our own vegetables and fruit, have our own chickens, but at the moment, we explained to Ned, we were not making use of the sea. As he downed another pint, he confidently claimed: 'Leave it to me!' I'll fix you a trammel net in that small bay of yours at the bottom of the cliff. That will give you fish every day of the week!'

This is how I described our trammel net:

The trammel net was fifty yards long, six feet deep, and had a two-inch mesh. Weights were fastened at intervals along one length of the net and corks along the other, specially balanced so that they floated six feet deep from the surface of the sea. Normally the net was used by either end being attached to two boats, so that they swept the sea like a mine-sweeper; but Ned's proposal was that we should adjust the principle to our particular conditions which demanded that we should 'shoot' the net from the rocks and use a buoy anchored in the little bay with a pulley attached. The net had long ropes at either end and one of these was threaded through the pulley, then brought back to the rocks . . . so that when we 'shot' the net we would haul one rope to send it out across the little bay, and haul the other when we brought it ashore, both ropes of course being at other times securely tied to the rings we had cemented in holes in the rocks.

For a couple of weeks the net was so successful that we lived on fish. Every day at low tide we would go down to the rocks, pull in the net and gather the harvest. We began selling fish to our neighbours. We had pollack and mackerel, and we would bring our catch back to the cottage where Monty was waiting to welcome us. We were thrilled that our investment of fifty pounds on the net was giving us such a splendid return. But it was only for two weeks. One night a ferocious gale blew up, and that was the end of the net.

The CID officers changed the direction of their talk. They began to tell me of the problems which beset them as they carried out their investigations, and as they talked I sensed they were leading up to the problems surrounding this immediate investigation. As if they were giving me a warning.

'We have many problems,' said one, 'apart from trying to catch the villain. The public thinks that is all we have to do, use our expertise to catch the villain. But there are all sorts of side issues which hamper us in our work.'

He went on to outline familiar examples: superiors who sit in offices, possessing power but out of touch with those who are working on the ground; the difficulties in securing convictions. He said that the law has in recent years become more and more in favour of the criminal at the expense of the victim. He cited the example of how a defence lawyer can now demand from a prosecuting police officer the name of the informant which enabled the charge against the villain to be brought. 'If we did that,' he said, 'our detection system could break down.' Then he added: 'Thus, in order to safeguard that system, we have to withdraw the prosecution case and the villain goes free. Many, many villains are circulating as free men and women because of technicalities of the law being on their side.'

He explained also about the frustration the police have at the sentences a criminal receives.

'We get a call that a burglary has been committed at such and such a house,' he said. 'We are on another job so we are late in getting to the house, whereupon we get a ticking off from the householder. We explain, and he calms down. We proceed to make our investigation, and in due course we may be lucky to identify the burglar. He is arrested, brought before the court and given bail until his trial proper begins, during which time, if he is a confirmed burglar, he will commit other burglaries. At last the arrested man comes up for trial and we have done much paperwork before that happens . . . all reports, for instance, have to be written by hand. Then there is the verdict. Often a villain is acquitted on a technical reason, and yet we *know* that he has committed the crime he is accused of. Then there is the frustration of sometimes seeing a villain who has been found guilty getting a sentence which is laughable.'

I sat there listening, wondering what this was leading up to.

'In this case of the cannabis down the cliff,' continued the officer, 'there are certain problems connected with what I have just said. Possession of cannabis, for instance, unless it is on a large commercial scale, is often viewed by magistrates as a minor offence and a modest fine will be the result. So we have done all the hard work, which has involved a lot of expense, work which has taken us away from other crimes, and we have virtually wasted our time.'

I sensed that he was warning me that the investigation might not continue because of the work and expense involved. And so I interrupted him.

'I think I must emphasize once again,' I said, 'that it is not just the growing of cannabis that is the crime. The real crime is stealing the use of my land, stealing the daffodil bulbs and, for that matter, putting my reputation at risk. After all, supposing an outsider, and not my own man, had discovered what was happening and had reported it to the police? Would not suspicion have fallen on me? These are the factors which enrage me. However long it takes I intend to identify the person concerned, and so I do hope you are not thinking of slowing down the investigation.'

Both officers were smiling.

'You've got it wrong,' one of them said, his smile becoming wider. 'We are stepping it up, not slowing down. What we have been trying to describe is what the public often doesn't realize . . . the cost, the time involved, the need to balance the value of one investigation against another, and always remembering that manpower is very limited.'

He paused.

I felt embarrassed that I had so misjudged them.

'I didn't mean to doubt your persistence,' I said lamely, adding: 'What do you mean by stepping it up?'

'We are going to place a microphone along the track to the meadows, and we are going to monitor it from six in the morning till ten in the evening. There will be two policemen, working in shifts, during that time.'

I reacted enthusiastically. Then I had second thoughts.

'It's a splendid plan,' I said, 'but does the operation cover the period when the villain might be operating? I mean wouldn't he avoid daytime, go there during the night and at dawn?'

'That's the sort of problem we are up against,' said the officer. 'The sort of problem which I tried to explain to you. It is the question of cost. The cost of night surveillance is very high. In such surveillances, regulations state there must be two officers on duty.'

'But the cost, surely, of surveillance at the wrong time is even more because there is little chance of getting a positive result?'

'That's nothing to do with us working on the ground. It is the decision of headquarters. They have calculated the cost of this mission and, apart from anything else, there is already the expense of the helicopter. You see, it is the cost of an investigation which dominates it.'

However I was a lucky one. The cost of the investigation had been assessed, and headquarters had sanctioned a microphone surveillance.

'How is it going to be operated?' I asked.

162

The CID officers outlined the plan.

The microphone would be lightly buried along the track to the meadows, but it wasn't an ordinary track. One had to have a countryman's eye to observe it, for grass, twigs and brambles covered its approach to the meadows. The microphone had to be so installed that its signal, should anyone pass near it, would echo back to a control post close to the cottage where the officer concerned would be on duty. Where should the control post be? Various sites were tested, but when the final one was chosen I had a rush of pleasurable adrenalin. It was Jeannie's studio . . . and so Jeannie was going to be a part of the search for the person who had cheated us.

The officers left and returned at six with two 'watchers'. The CID officers gave them a tour of where the microphone was hidden (which was not far from the coastal footpath) and introduced them to Jeannie's studio. I was with them when they came to it. It is a wooden hut, cunningly hidden within the granite stone walls of a long-ago, roofless building. It has a wonderful view through a gap in the walls of Carn Barges and the sweep of Mount's Bay. Within the studio there are the mementos, still in place, of when Jeannie last used it. There is her painting of Fred and Merlin against the background of the sea, still on her easel; and beside the easel are squashed tubes of paint which she used, and the brushes too. There is the schooldesk in a corner which she loved as a child and in a drawer of which I found,

after she died, the lines which she had never shown
me . . .

> The spirits of Minack
> Welcome you
> To their world of Forever
> Where life continues
> And death is never.

Scattered around the studio are the books she had collected as research material for her three hotel novels
and bundles of typewritten pages which she had discarded because they had displeased her. Jeannie was a
perfectionist.

And there is the table at which she sat, a pinewood
table which we had bought in Falmouth where she
typed her manuscripts and where she used patiently to
type the fair copy of my own books. The studio keeps
extraordinarily dry. There is no sign of damp. There
is a small armchair and a chest full of old newspapers and magazines, many of which have articles
referring to her and to Minack. It was this corner
of Jeannie's life which was now to be the headquarters
for the microphone surveillance exercise. Hanging
on the wall is her painting of Oliver and an etching
of Ambrose. They were peering out of their picture
frames as if they too were part of the surveillance
team.

The two heavily built policemen settled in, and I left
them there; and because it was a lovely May morning,
and it was so early, I took time off and went for a

nostalgic stroll around Minack. Bluebells were appearing in odd corners, showing between grey moss-covered rocks. Cow parsley was in profusion along the lane. A dazzling green fern shone in the shadow of the bridge. Nettles galore were growing in every space I had not cultivated. Bracken fronds were sprouting at racing speed in the field in front of the stable. A gull was on the roof. Bees were humming among the pink flowers of Escallonia Towers. The sweet scent of trichocarpa buds perfumed the air above the white seat. The cherry tree blossom hung in clusters. Across the valley the big field of Oliver land was swathed in celandines. An early morning that was so still that no tender leaf moved, and the sea stretching to the Lizard was as smooth as a vast pond.

I went back to the cottage, gave Cherry, who was sitting sphinx-like on a rock outside the porch, a dollop of tuna from a tin; then threw a couple of bread slices up to the gull and birdseed to the chaffinches, and finally helped myself to sliced peaches. Then I sat on the sofa, aimlessly thinking, just staring into space. There had been many lovely early May mornings at Minack like this one in our lives. There was the wonder of such early mornings when Jeannie and I would be up at dawn, hastening down to the top of the cliff where yesterday's potato digging was waiting to be weighed. Such a simple act, one might think, yet bliss in its fundamental pleasure. Such a contrast to the slick world we had left.

Ironic, therefore, that the life from which we had chosen to escape had come back to us on this Cornish cliff; and that the studio, which had remained safe with Jeannie's secret thoughts all these years, should have become the listening post to catch the perpetrator of this invasion of tranquillity.

I myself took no part in the surveillance. My role was to become friends with the policemen on their shifts, and to be ready to help them in any emergencies.

Soon after nine o'clock on that first morning, I was with the two policemen in Jeannie's studio when the alert note from the microphone rang out. Instantly the two policemen dashed out of the studio and down the path towards the white gate which cuts Minack off from strangers. I had, however, made a mistake. I had forgotten to warn the two policemen that the donkeys were in the stable field. Merlin and Susie are always looking for a diversion to brighten up their lives; and the sight of two large policemen dashing down the path was just the kind of diversion they were seeking. Thus I had been immediately faced with an emergency which I could not control. I just stood watching the scene, laughing and hoping the policemen would reach the white gate before the donkeys caught up with them. They did.

The emergency was a false alarm, but as I waited to hear this my mind went back to another occasion when a Minack donkey chased a visitor. Fred, the donkey of *A Donkey in the Meadow*, was the guilty one.

He and Penny were grazing in the big field where now runs the official coastal path. Jeannie and I were sitting on the white seat below the cottage when a large elderly lady came storming up the path from the field.

'Are those your donkeys?' she puffed out.

'Yes, what's wrong?'

'My husband and I were resting on the grass,' she said, 'when one of them came up to us . . . and snatched the cap my husband was wearing. It is now running round the field with the cap in its mouth!'

During the next few days the surveillance continued in the way I had anticipated. It was a pity. The two policemen who were on shift duty were repeatedly being warned by the bleep of the microphone that someone was in the neighbourhood of the microphone. They would repeatedly be dashing down the path to the white gate and the cliff field, only to find it was an innocent hiker. This daytime surveillance was valueless. It gave, however, pleasure to the policemen who were detailed to operate the surveillance.

'Such a change after the rough work which is our normal routine,' was the attitude. 'It is so beautiful here.'

Then I would listen to them talking about the frustration of their work, once again listening to the theme that, after a long investigation, they could produce a case against someone only to find that the accused is let off with a flimsy punishment.

167

'All that work for nothing', said one of the police-man, adding, 'And that attitude of the court is usually the response to someone accused of possessing cannabis.'

I waited a moment.

'But this case is different,' I said then, 'because if you can catch the man concerned redhanded it will mean a jail sentence. It is not just the growing of canna-bis which is the crime. It is the stealing of the land on which to grow it. It is the stealing of the daffodil bulbs. It is the fact that I could have been the person who could have been suspected of growing it. The villain concerned may have been deliberately using me as a cover.'

My friends did not need any persuading.

The days went by, and no one was caught red-handed. Then orders came from headquarters to with-draw the microphone. They would activate it again, possibly, nearer the cannabis harvest time during August.

A curious incident occurred during the night after they had told me the microphone surveillance was being withdrawn.

I was woken up just after dawn by a crescendo of bellows from Susie. Was she acting as a donkey microphone?

XI

I wanted to go round the world when I was nineteen but my parents thought it unwise. Nothing unusual in that. Nor was it unusual on my part that I wanted to gain experience of life outside my family environment, despite the environment being a happy one. I had to wait six years before a chance came which could not be refused. I had been writing a column in the *Daily Mirror*, and I was suddenly fired. Within a couple of hours of the shock I asked the editor if I could write one more column, and in the column I announced that I was going round the world. There could be no turning back.

I found in the Confusion Room the letters I had written to my family during my travels. My father had filed them, together with letters that my family wrote to me. It has been an odd experience touching again the letters I had written in faraway places.

The first letters from my family were not auspicious. I had been in New York, the first leg of my travels, for ten days. I had left debts behind me in London, and a letter from my brother Colin giving me details had gone astray. Thus I got this letter from my usually supportive mother:

I suppose you must have got Colin's letter by now telling

you the dismal figures. It seems a long time since he wrote but you have never replied.

It's all grossly careless of you because you ought to have known how things were. I know that it was carelessness; still *that* was wrong. It amazes me how entirely out of gear you were with your debts . . . you simply can't have attempted to look them squarely in the face of the difference between what you expected would be over, and the amount that *is* over.

I cannot remember the details of this financial situation. I remember, however, the mood I was in as the time drew nearer and nearer to my departure on my world journey. No logic must stop it, I was saying to myself. Yet logic was to hover around me for all the year to come. I was always to be crucially short of money . . . but time and again it was my family, who had criticized me for my carelessness, who were to rescue me.

They rescued me in New York where I had hoped to make money by writing about Britain, and I had an interview with the Hearst tycoon, though it came to nothing. But the life in New York was too much like the London life I had left . . . which is why, six weeks after arriving, I was on a Greyhound bus on a bumpy journey across America to San Francisco.

San Francisco had been a dream place for me ever since I was a child. My imagination weaved situations where I was with people who helped to light up every moment of my life. San Francisco was romance. I was fascinated by a connection that my family had with the famous earthquake of 1906. A great uncle was there at the time, and he wrote the most vivid description of what he saw and what he experienced. The letter was bequeathed to me, and I kept it on my desk for year after year. It is no longer there. Where has it gone? Was I idiot enough to send it to a researcher in Willowisck, Cleveland, Ohio, who was researching the earthquake, and who had heard I had the letter?

The letters to my family began after I arrived in San Francisco.

956 Sacramento Street
San Francisco

I have this very nice apartment, and it is a real little home. The only snag is that I have to suffer a stream of trams climbing up the steep hill beneath me. I keep very much to myself because I just can't afford to mix with people . . . but I had a brainwave last night and I'll tell you about it in a minute. This apartment looks over the rooftops of China-town. I haven't drawn the blinds and there is on my left the floodlit gold pagoda of a temple, and there is also a cross pencilled with lights. All very pretty.

Now about that brainwave. Gertie Lawrence is playing *Susan and God* at the Curran Theatre, and you know that she is a good friend of mine. I called in at the theatre a couple of evenings ago, and she gave me a wonderful greeting. Of course if I had been in London and was writing my column I would have asked her out to supper. Naturally I couldn't do that because I have been living on fruit, that's the cheapest kind of food. At the same time I have been giving the impression that I was still writing for the *Mirror* about my travels. So how on earth could I explain away any apparent lack of money? Here was the brainwave ... I told Gertie in her dressing room, and there were celebrities present, that I had lost all my money gambling in Reno during a three-day stay there on my way! I told it with such gusto that everyone seemed to believe me. Gertie thought it hugely funny. She asked me out last night after the theatre, and I had a marvellous time. The chief of the San Francisco police took us on a tour of Chinatown, and we had a detective with us. There was a hilarious incident. HMS *York* is here on a courtesy visit. Around one in the morning we were in Grant Avenue, and we were passing a taxi which had pulled up, and in it were a couple of seamen in their Royal Naval uniforms. Gertie ran to it, delighted to see these men from England. 'I am Gertie Lawrence!' she beamed. The seamen hadn't a clue who she was because they were so drunk. All they said was: 'Show where we can get some women.' She is the most enchanting person, seemingly scatterbrained and mad, but never missing a thing. She is off to play in Los Angeles next week, and has asked me to call at the theatre when I get there.

September 19th
San Francisco

Darlings,
The situation is a bit clearer, and Chamberlain seems to have saved civilization anyhow for a bit. Let's hope England now really buckles down to it and makes herself safe, because the war is certain to come. But Chamberlain has given us time to prepare. The *San Francisco Chronicle* has published an article I have written on these lines.

172

To non-serious matters. I am really pleased that I have made up my mind to go to Hollywood. I ought to be able to pick up a bit of money there writing. I'll be sorry to leave San Francisco, but it hasn't quite given me the opportunities I expected.

Blackburn Apartments
1805 Wilcox Avenue
Hollywood
October 2nd

This place is situated two hundred yards off Hollywood Boulevard about half a mile from the famous Brown Derby. From my window I can see the Santa Monica Mountains, which surprises me as I'd always imagined Hollywood to be on a large plain.

Gertie has been in Los Angeles and I've been out with her twice for supper. The first time last Monday I was in her dressing room when she came off stage. She threw her arms around me and then said: 'Why did they put all those aeroplanes over your article?' She was referring to the decorations around my *San Francisco Chronicle* Article. Apparently she had shown the article to all sorts of people, then she said: 'It really moved me.' We went out for supper with a man called Johnny Green who wrote my favourite song 'Body and Soul'. He is writing a new show for her. She knew him when he was very young, and he had come to her one day with four numbers including 'Body and Soul' which she adored. She gave him £50 for a quarter share, and she took it to Ambrose and sang it at the Mayfair. The result is history.

173

Blackburn Apart.
October 10th

I told you I met Mack Gordon and Gordon Revel in San Francisco. They are the song team who have written the Bing Crosby pictures, also Shirley Temple's, *Rebecca of Sunnybrook Farm* etc. I spent the day with them yesterday at Twentieth Century Fox studios. They are in the middle of a film called *Thanks for Everything*, and they were rehearsing the players. In came Binnie Barnes and Jack Oakie and Tony Martin, husband of Alice Faye. The place was bedlam. Jack Oakie, ferociously chewing gum with his hat on the back of his head, was telling everyone he had lost three stone. Gordon and Revel, delighted with their compositions, would play the same tunes time after time.

I met Shirley Temple just as she was going to the set after lunch, the film being the first technicolor she had done and called *The Little Princess*. She and her mother were staying in a bungalow close to the set. The mother is the sort of woman who on shopping expeditions would always get the best value at the cheapest price, she was so nicely unshowy and sensible. Shirley, of course, was entrancing. Amazingly natural. She had gone out of her bungalow, was getting into the car when she cried out: 'Oh heavens, my doll!' And rushed back to get it.

SS *Nyhorn*
November 5th

I am glad I have left Hollywood. I had a wonderful time, met so many of the stars, but it was all too frivolous. I feel that I am at last going to experience what away-from-it-all world travelling is really like.

174

I boarded the *Nyhorn* at San Pedro, and we are due to arrive at Panama in ten days' time. She is a comfortable boat of 3000 tons, loaded with a varied cargo of lead, zinc, canned fruits and lumber. I have a lovely cabin to myself with a window looking out on to the Pacific. It is capable of carrying eight passengers but there are only three others on board. One is an English-born Canadian who immediately told me he was on his way back to England to die. Mr Brown he is called. The other two are a tense young American prelate with the comic name of Figaro, and the third is a bishop, the Bishop of Panama, who speaks very broken English. It promises to be a very holy voyage. The Captain and the crew are Norwegian. Mr Brown, incidentally, is proving himself a bore. He is always saying to me: 'Let me tell you about my experiences in the Boer War.' Yes, a boor! Ten days of him will send me round the bend.

The Bishop discussed his weight at dinner last night, and also the weight of the rest of us. Mr Brown said he weighed 139 pounds but after being a week on the ship he was sure he had gone up another ten pounds. The Bishop said he was on a diet which had brought him down twenty-five pounds, and Mr Brown said he wished he had given the twenty-five pounds to him. Finally the discussion got so involved that the Captain said we should weigh ourselves, and as the only weighing machine was in the hold and was the one that weighed the meat, we all traipsed down there, the Bishop with dignity going first down the ladder followed by Figaro. The results rather spoilt the rest of the evening, and even today Mr Brown was a little quiet and the Bishop was quiet also. I weighed 152 pounds. Mr Brown, alas, instead of weighing more than his hoped-for weight, weighed nine pounds less; and the Bishop had told a little white lie as his twenty-five pounds was but fifteen pounds.

There was a full moon last night and a gentle warm breeze. Just as the sun was going down, a huge Californian hawk circled round the ship and came to rest on one of the ropes sloping down from the masthead. It stayed there all night and I could see its outline against the moonlit sky. Yes, I am feeling that at last I am beginning my *real* travels. Once in Panama I will go to Colon on the Atlantic side of the Panama Canal, where the Messageries Maritimes boat bound for Tahiti will dock after its voyage from Marseilles, and on which I am banking on getting a passage.

It is the last day on Board. There is a blue sky, a quiet sea. I am experiencing the pleasure of unknown adventures ahead, a freedom from the artificial world I have left. And I am beginning to form the theme of my book which I will write when my travels are over. Everybody dreams of travelling round the world, rich man or poor man. Many want to go because they believe that they will have experiences that will benefit them in later life. Others, who are old, because they were never able to go when they were young. They go for curiosity because it is too late for them to benefit from the experience very much. The theme of my book is what a year's travel has done to me, so that it can be held up as a mirror to all those who have wanted, and still want, to do the same.

SS *Ville d'Amiens*
December 4th

I'll be so glad when this voyage is over. I was lucky to get a place on board, but what a place! And it has only cost me

£10! But the conditions are awful. Of course it is steerage, and that means the straw mattresses are spread out deep in the hold. Everything is filthy, and last night I squished six black beetles crawling over me. The food is terrible, and I have been perpetually hungry. We are given the leftovers from the 1st and 2nd class passengers, and I've had no meat because it is always high. The stewards treat us like cattle, and we are not allowed to enter the 1st or 2nd class saloons even when I am invited by a passenger. The water tastes of rust. We eat off tin plates which haven't been washed, and our lunch is at 10.30 a.m. and our supper at 5.30 p.m. The crew is mostly French African, and when I had my feet resting on a bench, one of the Africans came up and shouted at me to take them off, as if I was his servant . . . Thank goodness the voyage will soon be over.

Papiare, Tahiti
January 1st

Dear family,
If I were someone with no ties, there is no doubt I would stay here for ever. Never have I known nor will I again an atmosphere so congenial and happy-go-lucky living. No one is worried by anything, and one can understand this because one just doesn't belong to the rest of the world. I seem to be on another planet and looking down on the world objectively. I can see quite plainly that the civilized world is mad. Quite screwy. Here is an attitude of laissez-faire. People mind their own business. Everything is primitive, everyone takes a long time to do anything, there is a lot of singing, a lot of dancing, a lot of laughter.
I have been staying with Mauu, a legendary Tahitian who

177

knew Rupert Brooke, and he said I was just like Rupert Brooke because I never can keep my *pareu* tight around my waist, just like Rupert Brooke! I went to see the hut where he lived but it is broken down now. But I met a man who knew him, and who knew the lovely Mamua who comes into his poems.

January 5th. I've made a big decision. I'm not going to take the *Tolten* for New Zealand that I had planned to take. I am captured by these islands. I've heard the most wonderful stories of the islands of Raiatea, Huahine and Bora Bora, and I'm going there tomorrow, going there in a sailing schooner.

January 10th. I have found the island of my dreams, across the lagoon from Bora Bora. I have a *faré* a few yards from the lapping water of the lagoon, and I am going to shut myself inside this island and forget the outside world. I will make notes for my book, but please don't expect any letters. I say that as if I've only got to write them and will be able to send them. That is of course rubbish. Only spasmodically does a schooner call here, and I can't even cable you because it is a very ancient wireless station and the man who works it is the local schoolmaster, and he has gone away to Papeete. And I don't want to think about writing letters because they represent a rope tying me to the outside world, and for a while I want totally to forget the outside world. Having said all that, I feel at peace. I hope you understand. Anyhow all that has happened will be in my book so you will catch up in due course. *Ia ora na* . . . which means 'good life to you'.

Suva, Fiji
February 27th

I mailed a letter on the day I left Bora Bora and my island of Toopua. In it I described the wonder of my stay, every moment of which I will treasure all my life. Now I have just disembarked from the *Stella Polaris*, and I can tell you something about my voyage aboard her. It was all so chaotic at the beginning. I had intended going back to Papeete, then sail in the *Tolten* to New Zealand. But the schooner which was to take me there didn't arrive. Apparently her captain had friends on an island where he had stopped to enjoy their company. Hence I was going to be too late to catch the *Tolten*. However the *Stella Polaris*, a cruise ship containing American millionaires, was due at Bora Bora, and I decided to try and get a passage aboard her. There was a big snag. I only had my basic things in a kitbag with me because I had left my trunk in Papeete, and the *Stella Polaris* was not going back there. She was going to Pago Pago, Rarotonga and Samoa then Fiji. Thus I would not be seeing my trunk again. And then there was all sorts of trouble about being allowed on board. The captain had looked at me and didn't think I would be a suitable passenger. I was, after all, looking like a traditional beachcomber. I was wearing only a *pareu* and I was barefooted. Luckily there was a man on board whom I had known in Hollywood, and he vouched for me. Even that required complicated negotiations, but I won't go into that now. I just want to say that I had a lot of fun on board. There were three specially attractive millionaire daughters, but I couldn't get serious with any of them because the ship was so small that there wasn't a corner where someone would not be watching. Nonetheless I was an outrageous success (forgive my conceit) because I brought life to the passengers who had been too long in each other's company. And here was this English beachcomber who was wandering about barefooted, and only a *pareu* around his middle! I had my reward in the end. Just before we moored in Suva, one of the lovely heiresses pressed an envelope into my hand, saying she wanted me to open it after the *Stella* had sailed. And when she did sail I quickly opened it, and there tucked neatly inside were two five-pound notes.

It was a long time after leaving Bora Bora and Toopua that I received this letter from my father:

I can't resist sending you a line on this your very last day in Tahiti for I know how you will be feeling. It is now about 4 a.m. with you, and you will have had your last dance, and in a few hours the farewell *tiaré* will be round your neck, and you'll be waving farewell and promising to return again. And if you are wise, you will never return again, for it will never be quite the same as this, your first visit. Many a time you will recall memories of the waving palm trees, the sighing of the sea on the reef, the fantastic shapes of the mountains, and the merry maidens' voices. And one day you will somehow and somewhere get a whiff of the scent of the coconut mingled with that of the *tiaré*, and in a flash you will suddenly be transported in spirit back to that happy isle. The memory of it will be a blessing to you for ever.

By the same post was a letter from my mother:

I had reminders of you today. A pair of socks found under your bed, and half a Toblerone in a drawer!

SS *Awatea*
March 16th

My stay in New Zealand was a success I think. I saw all the people you wanted me to see, and they were all so kind.

Wilfred [my uncle] is longing to get back to England, but he and Joyce are having difficulty in selling their house, and then there are Government restrictions about taking money out of New Zealand. But this letter is not about my stay. It is about your news of dear Lance which was in your letter I got before boarding this ship on the way to Sydney. I feel very sentimental, very sad. I loved him so much. Eight years since I told you that I longed for an Old English Sheepdog, and Daddy said he had business to do in Exeter and asked me to come with him . . . a subterfuge, because he had arranged to pick up this puppy at Exeter Station, and when we got there he took me into the guards van and there in a basket was Lance. What a moment that was for me! I will never have my games of hide and seek with him again, nor watch him hurtle past the sundial barking ferociously at imaginary trespassers, or hear that tiny squeak which seemed so strange coming from a big dog, nor see him clamber into the car whenever the door was open. I think of all the times we played together, walks to the Island, and the putting of him to bed in that old kitchen chair that only he found comfortable. Eight years since I first saw that little puppy. Eight years in the passing of which I made my debut in Lever Brothers, then my exit. That long time in Cranley Gardens, then Joubert Studios. Then that dreary wet night I arrived in Manchester to begin my new life on the *Daily Express*. Then London, and Paris and the articles I wrote for Schiaparelli. Debutante dances. Signing up for the *Daily Mirror*. All these things since those first days when Lance came into our lives.

Sorry to be so nostalgic! Will be in Sydney tomorrow.

Australia Hotel, Sydney
March 31st

I have had a lovely time in Melbourne but you will have got
my letter by now, and also about my short visit to Canberra.
Now I am back in Sydney, and busy getting everything organized for the next stage. I have put my writing things, photographs and typewriter in a kitbag and am sending it to New
York where it will join my trunk which I haven't seen since I
left Tahiti. My luggage is now reduced to my little Revelation suitcase, and the contents will be my only possessions
for the next two months. But I don't want to be cluttered
with baggage on this, the most exciting part of my travels
since I will be in anti-British countries like Japan and
Russia, let alone the last stage through Germany. Oh hell to
the Germans. War seems inevitable sooner or later. I've
done a lot of hard thinking as to what I should do, whether I
should stop my travels and immediately return home. But I
have a strange overwhelming instinct that I should continue.
It is an extraordinary driving force within me. No logic in it.
Don't worry abut me, darling Mum. I'm always better playing a lone hand, not being one of the crowd. Strange,
though, that I am sailing in a Japanese boat! She is a cargo
vessel called the *Kama Maru*.

SS *Kama Maru*
April 10th

It is proving to be a wonderful voyage. We have been sailing through the Torres Strait and the Arafura Sea. Last night when the moon peeped over the distant horizon and bathed the sea in an ethereal light, the sea that for two days has been as a pond on a summer's day, I thought of the wonderful nights I had on my island of Toopua. How lucky I have been. There are only ten passengers aboard. There is a German who has brought his family out of Germany because, though an Aryan, he is very anti-Hitler, or so he says. His family may be in Australia, but he is wandering around the Pacific without any apparent reason, and I have begun to suspect him. When he has a drink or two he becomes very pro his country. Then there is a Somerset Maugham character called Parkinson. He is going to Hong Kong to become chief engineer of a ship sailing the China Seas. He has had many adventures, has many stories to tell. One of them was so startling that I could not believe it to be true. He assured me it was. This is what he told me.

A diver called Bassett had gone up to the Persian Gulf on a job, from Sydney where he was based. While he was away his wife went off with a tea merchant who had a business trip to some port in Malaysia. On getting back to Sydney Bassett was immediately sent off to Albany Pass in northern Australia where a ship had been wrecked that had been carrying a quarter of a million pounds. It was lying in six fathoms, and Bassett succeeded in locating the safe containing the money, and the safe was brought to the surface. Before he left, however, Bassett, in his diving gear, had a look round, opening the doors of a couple of cabins. The first cabin was

183

empty. He opened the second cabin . . . and out floated a body which he immediately recognized. It was his wife. Around the neck was a pearl cross, pearls that were in the shape of a cross, and which he had given her on their wedding day. Bassett, horror-struck, snapped the life line which connected him with the rest of the crew on the surface, and would have died had it not been for their instant reaction. They saved his life, but not before, without the lifeline, the weight of the water had paralysed him from the waist down.

What do you think? Parkinson read my hand last night. I've always avoided having my future told, but he was very persuasive, and he told me how he had studied with famous fortune tellers. Anyhow he told me that my health will always be good, that I will be successful though I'll have to fight hard and sometimes I'll be really down, that the next two years were going to be really difficult but that in 1941 I'll have a success greater than I've ever had before. Then he said that my marrying year is 1943 or 4, that in the next twelve months a girl with the initial J or J.E. is going to be very important, and that my wife will be smaller than I, and dark.

There are no more of my letters in my father's file, except one. I do not know what happened to those I wrote from Manila, Hong Kong, Shanghai and Japan. The letter which was there had the heading in red type 'TRANS-SIBERIAN EXPRESS' and was the last letter I wrote before arriving home.

May 28th

We are just getting into Moscow. The journey across Siberia might have been a good deal worse but it was rather like travelling 5000 miles in a car without tyres. In my compartment I had two soldiers, a grandmother and a baby. Ten days of them were too much! I'll stay the night in Moscow, then go to Warsaw for a couple of nights, then on to Berlin for a couple. Then Paris and home . . . I have such a glorious time, and thank you, thank you all for the wonderful help you have given me.

I went to bed that night after reading the letters in a nostalgic mood; and I woke up at three o'clock in the morning (why is three o'clock in the morning such an active thinking time?), haunted by scenes in them. They were so vivid. Time, some people say, becomes a blur. I do not feel that way. Time, for me, is a plain, and I can suddenly recall in an instant all the emotions, all the environment, even a photographic image of those involved, of some incident of my youth. Thus I was lying there, content but nostalgic; and happy because I had realized what next I wanted to do in my unravelling of the Confusion Room. I was thinking about this next step, lying there in my small bedroom, the window facing down the lane, when I became aware of a noise which did not belong to the nighttime noise of a breeze touching the leaves of the trees, or the hum of a fishing boat on the way to Newlyn . . .

Then suddenly I heard the sharp rev of a car engine, followed by the dimmed lights of a car brushing the bedroom window. Why, at three o'clock in the morning, should a car be coming to Minack?

XII

I reacted by jumping out of bed and rushing to the window. The car – but I now saw it was a small van – had stopped in the space below the cherry tree. The engine had been switched off, so too the lights. I reacted, I believe, too quickly. I should have waited and seen who emerged from the van, but it was dark and I do not think I would have been able to identify who might be there. Thus I proceeded to bellow: 'What are you doing? Get out!' My bellow had an instant effect. The van's engine was restarted, the driver backed, swung round to the lane and hurtled away at speed across Monty's Leap.

The incident puzzled me. Was there a connection between it and the cannabis, which was nearly ready for harvesting? The gathering and the taking away of the plants was obviously going to be a problem for those concerned. The nearest car park was at Lamorna Cove, a mile away from the cannabis fields; and this would mean carrying the sacks that distance, and then someone might see them stuffing the sacks in the van. Yet why risk parking at Minack? Surely they knew I was there. Or did they believe that I would go on sleeping, and be unaware of what was happening?

In the morning I contacted a friend who lives in one of the cottages in the farm complex at the top of the lane, and he gave me some interesting information. He said he had heard the van pass his cottage, then when it reached the top of the lane where it begins to slope down to Minack the engine was cut off and the van freewheeled. I now realized that when I heard the noise of the sudden revving, the van had reached Monty's Leap and the driver had been forced to restart the engine. My friend added a curious postscript. He heard the van, as a result of my bellow, going at breakneck speed back towards the main road. Twenty minutes later, and by now it was half-past three, the telephone rang. 'Sorry, wrong number,' the caller said. A peculiar coincidence that there should be such a call at such a time. I reported the incident to the CID, and they said they would be out to see me within the next few days. They added they would have some news for me.

My three o'clock in the morning idea, before my happy thoughts were interrupted by the van, was to comb my diaries and notebooks in the Confusion Room for the quotations which have helped to influence my life. Since I was at school I have copied out quotations from books I have read and which have stirred my mind. I proceeded to search for the diaries and the notebooks, which I knew were somewhere and which for a long time had not been read by me.

As I searched I came across bundles of old gramophone records, and the sight of these set my thoughts at a tangent. I thought of the occasion when Roy Plomley, creator of *Desert Island Discs*, invited me to be his guest castaway on his mythical desert island. I spent six months beforehand trying to choose the eight favourite pieces of music required, and a great deal of time ever since thinking of the eight records I might have chosen. Roy Plomley was a very gentle person, and this is what helped to make his programme so popular. He interviewed celebrities from all over the world, probing their inside feelings, relaxing them, and so it was always fascinating to hear what records they had chosen. When he wrote his book *Plomley's Pick*, he surprisingly chose me as one of his fifty favourite castaways. Jeannie was so thrilled by this that she bought a magnum of Moët et Chandon as a celebration, which we drank alone together. Jeannie was always ready to celebrate a special moment.

The records I decided upon were these:

1. The Shepherd Boy's song which begins Act III of Puccini's *Tosca*.
2. '*Reflets dans l'Eau*' by Debussy, played by Walter Gieseking.
3. The Gallop from Bizet's *Jeux d'Enfants*.
4. 'I Dream of Jeannie with the Light Brown Hair' by Stephen Foster, played by Carroll Gibbons and his Orchestra.
5. The Adagio from Rachmaninov's Second Symphony, played by the London Symphony Orchestra conducted by André Previn.
6. The Finale of Haydn's String Quartet in D Major, Op. 78, No. 5.
7. The Prelude to Grieg's Holberg Suite, Op. 40, played by the Northern Sinfonia Orchestra conducted by Paul Tortelier.

8. 'This is My Lovely Day', music by Vivian Ellis and words
   by A. P. Herbert, sung by Georges Guetaray and Lisbeth
   Webb, from the musical *Bless the Bride*.

The records I would now like to have chosen are
legion, but does not this represent one of the problems of today? So much music to listen to, so many
beautiful places to go to, so many books to read, so
much media nonsense to waste one's time upon, so
much brainwashing television trivializing the reality of
life. I will not list my alternative records because the
list is too long. I leave it to you to make your own list.

And now here are my random collected quotations:

She was in her middle twenties and she had a quality of
generosity that I have found in few women. I mean, her
spirit came out to meet you, and you were aware of an
absence of bodily prudery that was unusual and delightful.

HOWARD SPRING, *Oh Absolom My Son*

Perhaps Dermot will come with me. We shall say goodbye to
you together, to you and to Rory . . . and remember the night
before either of you were born when in pride and blindness,
we told the years what they should do with our sons.

HOWARD SPRING, *Oh Absolom My Son*

The glow of the neon lights blushing the buildings, the fairy
lights of the skyscrapers, and all of them silhouetted against
an almost purple coloured darkness.

D.T., New York

Aye look: high heaven and earth all from the prime
    foundation,
All thoughts to rise the heart are here; and all are vain:

189

Horror and scorn and hate and fear and indignation.
Oh why did I awake? When shall I see sleep again?
Be still, be still my soul, it is but for a season:
Let us endure and see injustice done.

A. E. HOUSMAN

Lest I should know you too easily
You play with me.
You blind me with flashes of laughter to hide your tears.
I know, I know your art,
You never say the word you would.
Lest I should not praise you, you
elude me in a thousand ways.
Lest I should confuse you with the
crowd, you stand aside.
I know, I know your art.
You never walk the path you would.
Your claim is more than that of others,
that is why you are silent.
With playfulness you avoid my gists,
I know, I know your art,
You will never take what you would.

TAGORE, 'The Gardener'

Whoever shall attain the goal of Wisdom
Will shut his lips for good on where and why.
The Camel-bell relapses into silence
When once we reach the Caravan Serai.

A verse from the Persian poet TALIB KALINS,
Poet Laureate to the Emperor, Shah Johan

Why did he love her? Curious fool, be still!
Is human love the fruit of human will?

LORD BYRON

For it is the fidelity of the heart alone that I value.

MANONLESCAUT

Dying was nothing and he had no picture of it nor fear of it in his mind. But living was a field of grain blowing in the wind on the side of a hill. Living was a hawk in the sky. Living was an earthen jar of water in the dust of the threshing with the grain flailed out and the chaff flowing. Living was a horse between your legs and a carbine under one leg, and a hill and a valley and stream with trees along it and the far side of the valley and the hills beyond.

ERNEST HEMINGWAY, For Whom the Bell Tolls

Political conviction does not justify the distortion of truth.

MICHAEL SADLER

By unrighteousness men prosper, gain what they desire and triumph over their enemies, but at the end they are cut off at the root and suffer extinction.

TAGORE, Sadhana

Now, already sensually mature, you have fallen in love. The heavens have opened to you when you are equipped to appreciate them. I envy you the experience. I fell deeply in love before I was a man. The heavens opened before I had even watched a lady brush her hair.

CHARLES MORGAN, The Voyage

Near the snow, near the sun, in the highest fields
See how these names are fêted by the waving grass
And by the streamer of white cloud
And whispers of wind in the listening sky.

191

The names of those who in their lives fought for life,
Who wore at their hearts the fire's centre.
Born of the sun they travelled a short way towards the
    sun,
And left the vivid air signed with their honour.

STEPHEN SPENDER

> Stay, O sweet, and do not rise;
> The light that shines comes from thine eyes;
> The day breaks not, it is my heart,
> Because that you and I must part.
> Stay, or else my joys will die
> And perish in their infancy.

JOHN DONNE

These are the golden days. Every minute without her is a
minute lost. These are the days of discovery. When I lived
with her I knew so little of her, took so much for granted.
Now I feel the exultation of loving her and being loved by
her. These are the golden days.

D.T.

> Sometimes in wintry Springs
> Frost, as a midnight breath,
> Comes to the cherry flowers
> And blasts their prime.
> So I with all my powers
> Unused on men or things
> Go down the wind to death
> And know no fruiting time.

JOHN MASEFIELD

The production of a work of art is not the result of a miracle. It requires preparation. The soil, be it ever so rich, must be fed. By taking thought, by deliberate effort, the artist must enlarge, deepen and diversify his personality. Then the soil must lie fallow. Like the bride of Christ, the artist waits for the illumination that shall bring forth a new spiritual life. He goes about his ordinary business and then, suddenly springing, you might think from nowhere, the idea is produced. But like the corn that was sown on stony ground it may easily wither away; it must be tended with anxious care. All the power of the artist's mind must be set to work on it, all his technical skill, all his experience, and whatever he has in him of character and individuality, so that with infinite pains he may present it with the completeness that is fitting to it.

SOMERSET MAUGHAM, *The Summing Up*

Could we but live at will upon this perfect height,
Could we but always keep the passion of this peace,
Could we but face unshamed the look of this pure light,
Could we but win earth's heart, and give desire release
Then were we all divine, and then were ours by right
These stars, these nightingales, these scents, then shame
    would cease.

LIONEL JOHNSON, 'Bagley Wood'

His being was in her alone:
And he not being, she was none;
They joyed one joy, one grief they grieved.
One love they loved, one life they lived.
The hand was one, one was the sword,
That did his death, her death afford.
As all the rest, so now the stone
That tombs the two is justly one.

SIR PHILIP SIDNEY, 'EPITAPH'

Oh thou art fairer than the evening air
Clad in the beauty of a thousand stars.

CHRISTOPHER MARLOWE

Let's couple the future of England with the past of England. The glories and victories and triumphs that are over, and the sorrows that are over too.

Let's drink to our sons who made part of the pattern and to our hearts that died with them.

Let's drink to the spirit of gallantry and courage that made a strange Heaven out of unbelievable Hell, and let's drink to the hope that one day this country of ours, which we love so much, will find dignity and greatness again.

'The Toast' from NOËL COWARD, *Cavalcade*

Reverie is the groundwork of creative imagination. It is the privilege of the artist that with him it is not as with other men an escape from reality but the means by which he accedes to it. His reverie is purposeful.

SOMERSET MAUGHAM, *The Summing Up*

Why should you think that beauty, which is the most precious thing in the world, lies like a stone on the beach for the careless passer-by to pick up idly? Beauty is something wonderful and strange that the artist fashions out of the chaos of the world in the torment of his soul. And when he has made it, it is not given to all to know it. To recognize it you must repeat the adventure of the artist. It is a melody that he sings to you, and to hear it again in your own heart, you need knowledge and sensitiveness, and imagination.

SOMERSET MAUGHAM, *The Moon and Sixpence*

A blessed thing it is for any man or woman to have a friend, one human soul whom we can trust utterly, who knows the best and worst in us, and who loves us in spite of all our faults, who will speak the honest truth to us while the world flatters us to our face and laughs at us behind our back, who will give us counsel and reproof in the days of prosperity and self-conceit, but who again will comfort and encourage us in the day of difficulty and sorrow, when the world leaves us alone to fight the battle as we can. It is only the great hearted who can be true friends. The mean and the cowardly can never know what true friendship means.

CHARLES KINGSLEY

I had been going along like a tin of mixed biscuits (the image is before me now!), my mind choked with an assortment of feelings I had never got to the truth or meaning of. I was packed with experiences I had neither sized up nor turned to intelligent account. I had never even taken stock of my mental store. And it was only when I began to write to you that I found my feelings turning into ideas, and my experiences becoming luminous under the light of reflection. They then began to show answers that were the beginnings of wisdom, or at least of real knowledge. I began to see where I stood in relation to persons and things. I no longer sat in darkness, a sphinx to myself.

ACTON REED, *A Modern Document*

Against stupidity, the Gods themselves labour in vain.

GOETHE

Somerset Maugham, certainly, had a special impact on my life, but it was the French writer Marcel Proust with his masterpiece *Remembrance of Things Past* who opened the windows of my mind. I was introduced to his writing when I was nineteen years old, when I was full of inhibitions and puzzlement, and the sense of inadequacy. The windows opened and I found the distress I harboured did not belong to me alone. I found that his writing, describing his own journey of self-discovery, was the same journey that I wanted to follow. He gave me a motivation that excited me. I would try to lead my thinking life in the same way, trying to reveal my secret thoughts so that I could unravel the complications which beset me. Other writers were to help me on the journey, but it was Marcel Proust who fired the starting gun. He made me realize that the only writers I wanted to read were those who stirred my mind.

In a drawer of Labour Warms I found the notebook in which I had copied out passages from *Remembrance of Things Past*, subtle passages which were to make me say to myself: 'I feel like that but until now I could not put my feelings into words.'

There were passages which, as a nineteen-year-old at the beginning of a love affair, helped me to understand my dilemmas, helped me to understand the contradictions of a love affair. Proust's love affair with Gilberte was a tantalizing revelation. Swann's love for Odette was a mirror of agonizing frustration.

It is wonderful [I wrote in *Sun on the Lintel*] to have such a secret guide to the peculiar emotions of love. I was now free from the hitherto black and white moods which my solid upbringing had taught me to expect in my relationships with girls. You love her, or you don't love her. You want to sleep with her, or you don't. I was no longer to be held by the invisible reins of reason. I now knew that others felt with the same complexity as I sometimes felt. My doubts, conflicts within myself, confidence at one moment, fear of what the girl may be thinking of me making me dumb at the next, were not, as I now learnt, the unique feelings of myself. Proust, at that stage of life, provided me with the education that I required.

In another part of the drawer I found the diary about the beginnings of my life with Jeannie.

I have been appointed to organize a Press Section for MI5. My brief is to collect information which mirrors the gossip of newspaper correspondents of all nationalities and to assess their value, along with other tasks which I must keep secret and not put into my diary. I am to have an organization of my own, and I have been allocated a flat in Dolphin Square so I can operate independently of Head Office. It is an enormously important job because it covers so many areas, and I am very lucky because I am really excited since I conceitedly believe they have chosen just the right person!

I had such encouragement today. The Director General called me in to say that the work I was doing, the gathering of the mood and the unpublished stories of international newspapers, had attracted the attention of the Secretary of the War Cabinet, and he said that henceforth I would not just report at a weekly meeting to the Heads of MI5, but I also would report to the Secretary of the War Cabinet, Sir Edward Bridges, at a weekly meeting with him. Apparently he will sift the information I give him, and pass on to Churchill any item he thinks Churchill would be interested in.

I've been having the jitters. I have such a responsible job, and I get the same nervous strain as when I was writing a daily column. I am rushing around, seeing so many people, getting back late, waking up in the morning feeling awful. I need stability in my life. I need a girl, an understanding girl, but where can I find one? I don't know any girl who would be right.

I saw Jean Nicol today, the first time since I had dinner with her after she had put my book on the Savoy bookstall and she had told me her initials were J.E. She is a nice girl, far too young one would have thought to be in charge of the publicity of the Savoy Hotel Group, very pretty, but nothing sensational. A very conventional upbringing I should guess.

My job takes me often to the Savoy because it is such a meeting place for the well-informed. I was there last night when it was bombed. The bomb landed on the bedrooms facing the Strand, and three people were killed. The front hall was a shambles in the morning, and I was standing there in the midst of it when I saw Jean Nicol standing by the battered entrance. She looked so cool and collected, and she was talking to a group of American war correspondents. When she saw me she waved at me, then came over to me and asked me if I would like a drink. Of course I said yes, and she took me with a couple of American correspondents, one from the *New York Times*, the other from the New York *Herald Tribune*, to Room 205, which is her office. I was very impressed the way, in a very feminine fashion, she was in command of the situation. She looked so fragilely young.

I have been seeing Jeannie (I explained to her that I thought Jean was too formal). She gave me lunch yesterday in the Grill, and everyone made such a fuss of her. The editor of the *Daily Mail* joined us for coffee and a brandy, which was very useful for me because of my work. I picked up a lot of useful information.

What strikes me about Jeannie is her quickness of mind. She can adjust herself to each person she meets, so that the person feels at ease. She is doing such a valuable job, not just for the Savoy, but also for the American war correspondents whom she can help in many different ways, and this steers them into writing newspaper reports back to the States which favour Britain.

I like her very much, and I expect I'll be seeing her quite a lot because the people she sees are the people I want to mix with. I have asked her out to my weekly lunch gathering at Cholmondley House on Sunday. She stays at the weekend with her parents at St Albans, but she says she can manage to get away. Frankly I can see she can be very useful. I've got interesting people coming to lunch including Bondarenko, the Soviet chief of the Tass London Bureau, Claud Cockburn, the columnist of the *Daily Worker* and author of the notorious *The Week*, and Milan Gavrilovic, designate Prime Minister of a future Yugoslavia. There will also be Bill White of the New York *Herald Tribune*, Charlie Smith of the Hearst Organization, and Ronald Hyde, news editor of the London *Evening Standard*. Jeannie will act as hostess.

For six weeks running Jeannie has been coming to the Sunday lunches, wonderful for me to have such a hostess because everyone loves her. Robert St John, the London chief of the National Broadcasting Company, did a broadcast about these lunches to America the other day. He said: 'At Richmond on a Sunday you can meet a fascinating collection of people, Conservatives, Communists, Liberals, War Correspondents, newspaper editors, leaders of exiled European countries.

They are the new generation. Young people with vision and hope, thrashing out new ideas for building a brave new world.'

I gave Jeannie a topaz necklace today. She was thrilled. I got it at Solarios in Duke Street.

Friends have started to take as natural that Jeannie and I should always go around together. Yet I am still on guard. I say to myself that I can never expect to see again a girl like her . . . very pretty, clever in a practical fashion, very sensitive, a knowledge of public affairs, a knowledge of art and literature, and she is never at a loss in conversation with whomever it might be, and a delicious sense of humour: and besides all these things I believe she loves me . . . (I have now ennobled her as an M15 agent).

In my role as Jeannie's boss, I gave her today a delicate assignment, and I expect there will be more such assignments. There is an American correspondent at the Savoy who has just arrived via New York from Berlin where he has spent the first eighteen months of the war [America at the time being neutral]. MI5 want to know his views on the Berlin situation, and more especially whether he *might* be acting as an agent for the German Secret Service. When I outlined to Jeannie what I wanted her to do, she replied cheekily: 'Does that mean I have to go to bed with him if need be?'

My mother and father and my two brothers all adore Jeannie without reservation. Nigel says I must marry her, but I don't want to marry anyone at the moment. I want to remain free.

I'm getting on hellishly slowly with my Empire book *One King*. It is a nightmare. I've had to squeeze in interviews and research in between all my normal work, and then I have to start writing when I get home at night, working often to two or three in the morning. No one expects me ever to finish it except Jeannie. She never fails to encourage me.

Jeannie said today: 'It's so easy to take a side road from the main one and go down it a little way, and find oneself in a jungle one cannot get out of.'

What stops me from asking her to marry me? I suppose the real answer is my selfishness, no not quite selfishness but my unwillingness to shut the door on frivolous affairs, sudden romances which don't mean anything except their novelty and temporary acute excitement. In the next few months I'll have to make up my mind. Mind you, she likes her independence too, and she also may want to keep it. I don't think it is any use hurrying me into a decision. It will come suddenly.

May 15th 1943

I've had a very emotional day. Yesterday I had a call from a Polish friend in the Polish Secret Service, asking me to see him, saying he had with him a Polish secret agent who had arrived from Warsaw on behalf of the Polish Underground Movement. He had a terrible story to tell, my friend told me, and I could be of great help. I agreed to meet him. His name is Jan Karski, and he had indeed a terrible story to tell, not only of his own adventures as a Polish secret agent, but of the staggering horror that the Polish Underground had sent him to London to tell. He wanted it publicized, and this was why I was asked to help.

Today I organized a lunch with Ronald Hyde of the *Evening Standard* and Freddie Kuh, London chief of the American Associated Press. The lunch was in one of those cubicles in Simpson's Restaurant in the Strand, a cubicle where we could talk freely. Kuh, however, arrived when the lunch was nearly over. At first he was just a cynical

201

newspaperman, and he irritated me, as Karski began to tell his story, by mindlessly tapping the table with his pen. Then, as the story developed the tapping stopped. The horror of the story had sunk through Kuh's cynical mind, and his attention was captured. As soon as the meeting was over I went back to my office flat in Dolphin Square, and dictated to my secretary, Esther Whitfield, what I had heard.

Karski began his story by telling us of the warning the Head of the Polish Underground gave him before he left on his mission. He said that although your task is to tell the British and the Americans that they must make reprisals if any Jew in Poland is to survive, they will not believe your story. The officials will listen politely but they still will not understand . . . you will be pleased you have been invited to see them, and will have arrived at the office at half past eleven in the morning. You will give them all the evidence, you will be getting eloquent, you will be saying what we want done if we are to be saved . . . then at quarter to one your listeners will glance at their watches and one of them, to the delight of the others, will say it is lunchtime, and the interview will be over. They will not understand.

Of course there are reasons why they cannot understand. The war has to be pursued, the Second Front is being planned, and resources are limited. What strategic advantage would be gained by acceding to the Polish Underground request? Then Karski proceeded to give us, as we sat in the cubicle of Simpson's restaurant reasons as to why something should be done if there was to be any dignity left in the human race.

Karski has been three times smuggled out of Poland, and he described the kind of assignments in which he had been involved. Some successful, some disastrous, but all destined to get the evidence of the horror that the Gestapo was inflicting on the Jewish population.

He was ordered to try and get a Polish Jew Colonel and his wife out of a concentration camp. He succeeded with false papers in doing so. A week later, on the orders of the Gestapo, all the Jews in the camp were murdered as a result.

In July 1942 Himmler declared he had a special message from Hitler that all Jews must die but that they must die suffering as they were the cause of the war. Karski described one system that was used.

There was a wooden passage leading to a railway station. Thirty wagons were entrained there. At a signal the Gestapo started shooting. Each wagon had room for forty people. The Jews in a panic rushed down the wooden passage into the wagons. The Gestapo continued to shoot. The train shuddered with their cries. The doors were shut, but the horror did not end there. The Gestapo had covered the floors with lime. Fumes filled the wagon. The Jews died . . . lingeringly.

Karski was ordered to see for himself what was happening in the camp so that he could tell those in London when he got there an account which came from his personal experience. Somehow he got himself smuggled into a camp. He saw an elderly man, naked, sitting by himself. No one took any notice. He saw a dead baby. No one took any notice. He saw a young girl lying naked on the ground with her feet and hands tied to stakes. No one took any notice. He had other such terrible stories to tell. They were heartrending.

That evening, I remember, I gave Jeannie an account of the Karski story, and I remember how she had burst into tears when I had finished.

It was only years later did I realize that those tears were the first to be shed in the West for the horror of the Holocaust.

We are engaged! And the way I suddenly asked her was so funny. She had a date in the American Bar of the Savoy with a famous radio personality, and for some reason she didn't want me to meet him. So I said I would wait for her in the Coalhole, the pub next door to the Savoy, and she promised she would be there at half past six . . . half past, a quarter to seven, seven o'clock, and still no sign of Jeannie. At quarter past seven she appeared, looking delicious and holding a rare bottle of Savoy whisky which she handed me. She was very contrite. 'I thought this bottle would make up for being late,' she said, expecting me to be in a furious mood. She therefore did not expect my question: 'Will you marry me?' And without any hesitation she said yes. Later we had dinner with my father who was of course delighted. Then Jeannie, looking at my father, said: 'You know, when he asked me, anyone could have knocked me over with a tap!'

We were married at 12.15 p.m. in the little chapel nearest the main chapel in Richmond Parish Church. Jeannie was looking lovely in white and wearing the Dudley family veil which Patricia Ward had lent her. Just the families were there, and Colin was best man. The Reverend Harold Gray took the service which was very short. As Jeannie came into the church, the organist gave an imperfect rendering of 'Jerusalem', and as she came up the aisle, Colin whispered to me: 'Give her a winning smile!' We are both very, very happy.

I had closed the diary. Here I was in the Confusion Room, the door open, just as it was when I first began unravelling the contents . . . and once again I heard a car approaching, a police car again. But this time there were two cars. I wondered why.

XIII

The two CID officers who had become my friends were in the first car. In the second were two burly policemen who had been among the team who had monitored the microphone.

'I hope you won't be upset,' said one of my friends, 'but we have had orders from headquarters to abort our investigation. We ourselves would have liked it to continue, but our orders are clear. We are to pull up the cannabis plants and remove them.'

We were standing by the stable in front of the cherry tree. At that moment Merlin and Susie emerged from inside the stable and began to whinny. Doubtless they were hoping the police were visitors who had brought them carrots.

'That's a pity,' I said, and I found myself surprisingly calm. Then I added: 'Does this mean that after all these months you still do not know who the culprit may have been?'

My two friends looked at each other. Then one of them said: 'Yes, we know the culprit, but there is not enough evidence to start a prosecution.'

'But,' I interrupted, 'surely if we waited just a week or two longer we might catch him redhanded harvesting the cannabis?'

There was a pause.

'Two reasons why we can't. One is that we believe that the culprit has been tipped off about the investigation, and that has caused headquarters to make the decision. The second is a reasonable one. The culprit has had his punishment. He has worked all these months growing the cannabis, and he isn't going to earn a penny from it.'

'I see the point, but that doesn't compensate me for the emotional turmoil all this has caused me.'

'We understand, but there is nothing more that we can do.'

I suppose I should have been angry. I would have been angry if a kind of tiredness had not taken place in my mind. I realized I was like a long-distance runner who had come towards the end of his race. His energy had been burnt up, just as my emotional energy had been burnt up. True, I will always continue to simmer with anger, but to simmer is different from allowing one's anger to become an obsession. 'Beware of obsession,' an aunt of mine once warned me, 'because obsession can destroy the soul.' I found myself, therefore, reacting in docile fashion to what my friends had told me.

'All I can say,' I murmured, 'is to thank you for the work you have done. I'm sorry I have given you all this trouble for nothing.'

One of them smiled.

'You don't have to think that,' he said. 'Coming out here has been a great experience . . . and the team who monitored the microphone say it was the best assignment they have had in years. Isn't that so?'

He turned to the policemen in the second car.

'You're right,' was the answer. 'To work here in this beautiful place was like a holiday.'

The two Lager Louts had flown on to the roof, and were squawking.

'We will go down now,' went on my friend, 'and take the microphone from its hiding place, then pull up the plants and pack them in these bags. We'll take them back to the police station and burn them.'

They remained at Minack for another two hours. They collected the microphone, dismantled the equipment in Jeannie's studio, filled the cannabis plants into sacks and placed them in the second car, and were about to set off when I shouted: '*Stop!*'

Cherry had recently developed an extraordinary eccentricity of taking no notice of a moving car. Hence when I have got into my Volvo and am wishing to back it from the garage, I am stopped from doing so by an unmovable Cherry who is unperturbed by an approaching back wheel. The same thing happens when I am returning to Minack. I cross Monty's Leap, see the little black lump on the gravel between the white seat and the cherry tree, and the lump refuses to move. I approach nearer and nearer, blowing the horn, revving my engine, and Cherry still won't budge, looking at the Volvo with a baleful stare. This is what happened now. She was within a few feet of one of the CID cars, glaring at the driver as though challenging him to advance upon her . . . or perhaps, in this case, it was a form of protest against the failure to punish the person who had caused so much distress.

I watched the two cars disappear up the lane, across

Monty's Leap, then on past the corner where stands Jeannie's sign A PLACE FOR SOLITUDE; and as they disappeared out of view, the thought crossed my mind that my distress of the past few months was of minnow importance. All over the world beautiful places are being vandalized. There is the greed of the developers who choose a lonely, untamed coastline and vandalize it with a monstrous hotel, filling the hotel with mindless philistines. There is the developer who obeys the cries for housing estates, bulldozing the fields and the woods and destroying the peace of those who have long lived there. Then there are the ethnic wars achieving no object except a murderous macabre victory over a neighbourhood where, over the years, people had lived happily together. The casualties of these ethnic wars do not end with the suffering of the human population. The animal population suffers. Cats and dogs are also victims who have lost the safety of their homes.

I went back to the cottage and opened a bottle of Alsace wine. I felt unexpectedly relieved. The daily stress was over. There were not to be any prolonged worries such as, had they caught the culprit, a prosecution case in the courts. It was all over. I could now wake up in the morning and revel, without an underneath worry, in the joys of the day.

I do not feel lonely when I am alone. I never want to fill my life staring at television for the sake of its company. I never want to mix with people just for the sake of mixing with them. My life is so full that I can never catch up with the tasks I ought to be doing. Perhaps this is due to the fact that I am not a natural 'doer'. I prefer to sit and contemplate. I prefer my mind to be idle. Thus I am amazed as to how I have written my books. How, for instance, had I the concentration and the stamina to write the 180,000 words of my book on the British Commonwealth called *One King*? I am flummoxed. Each time I have put a blank piece of paper in my typewriter and typed 'Chapter One', I have been appalled. How am I going to find the words for *that* page, let alone the pages of a whole book?

Of course there are moments of sadness, even of despair, but they are passing phases. No one who lives at Minack could have these moods for long. One doesn't need a counsellor to remove them, no need to lean on his or her shoulder for support. The support must come from within oneself, nurtured and blossomed by the beauty of creation within an untamed countryside.

Cherry had joined me. She had jumped on my desk, then leapt on to the small dining table, from there to the old oak chest–knocking over a signed photograph of Churchill in the process – and then a final leap to the Sheraton table where I was sitting. I never understand why she cannot use the floor as a means of going from one place to another.

I am inclined to over-concern myself about Cherry. I do not, at the moment, find any reason to fret about her health, but when the vet came out to deal with a pebble which had become lodged in Susie's front foot, I asked him to give Cherry a check. I have become influenced by those medical pundits who, in order to lure your attention, issue warnings that although you may feel wonderfully well you may have something wrong with you.

Cherry was wonderfully well, but I thought it wise to take advantage of the vet's presence. 'She behaves like a kitten,' I said to him, 'and is tremendously active.'

The vet checked her and pronounced her to be in splendid condition.

This should have satisfied me, but the good news opened up another reason to worry, a worry which has persisted during all the years that Cherry has been alone with me since Jeannie and Ambrose died. I have been her only companion, her slave who adores her. My worry was simply this: supposing something befell me, what would happen to Cherry? I might break a leg, go to hospital. Who would care for Cherry after I had gone? Then I would sometimes wonder who it was who cared for her at the beginning of her life. Who was it who first saw her as a little black kitten? Who was it who had loved her, then suffered the agony of her disappearance? When she came to Minack and Jeannie found her one foggy day beneath the cherry tree, the then vet said she had been spayed about six months previously. Where had she been? How did she find the way to Minack? Had she perhaps got into a van and the driver, unaware of his passenger, had driven many miles to this area of Cornwall and Cherry had escaped when the van doors were opened? Despite all our enquiries, no resident in this area had lost a little black cat.

She was now looking up at me from the floor.

'All right,' I said, 'I know what you are wanting.' And I got up from the sofa, went to the kitchen and prised open a tin of Whiskas.

She dipped her nose into the saucer, and I took the opportunity to leave her. I did not want Cherry to follow me up the lane. I had an impulse to see the donkeys, and I did not want to be delayed by a languid Cherry walk.

I passed the Confusion Room door. I had to admit to myself that the unravelling of its contents was not complete. Indeed it could continue for a very long time and still not be completed. Yet the unravelling which had taken place had done much to unravel the confusion of my mind. I was able to see the past in perspective. I had lived again periods of my life and had been able to ponder about the decisions I had made, to ask myself whether I would have acted differently had I been faced with those decisions years later. I do not think I would have acted differently except on minor occasions. I am not a logical person and I have never worked to a plan. I have acted through instinct, and I have often had the luck to meet the right person at the right time. Luck is a vital ingredient. One only has to look around to witness the bad luck so many people have to endure. When Jeannie and I decided to leave our London lives, we did not make the decision logically. We just felt it was our destiny, a destiny that was pushing us, a driving force within ourselves which was so strong that it defeated all the logical reasons why we should not leave, and led us to a new life of growing potatoes and flowers about which we knew nothing. But it was luck that was our passport. The luck of finding Minack when it was empty and deserted, the luck of the timing that the owner was trying to find an occupier.

I had learnt, out of the unravelling, one certain lesson: keep a diary. I do not mean a diary that dominates you, making you feel guilty if you do not enter your thoughts and doings every day, or every week – or even every month. The purpose of a diary is for it to act like a ladder in your life. It should reflect the highs and lows, the clues which slowly enable you to understand your life, what emotions steered you, reminding you of incidents that you had long forgotten. A diary gives the satisfaction of being able to look back so that your life is not hidden in a fog. It is with you, an alive memory force . . . and then you find, as I have done, that basically you never change.

I wended my way across Monty's Leap. There is now wedged on the edge of the lane, beneath where Monty is buried and where the little stream passes it, a block which was once a harsh piece of cement, and upon which is inscribed 'MONTY'S LEAP'. The block was given us by an engraver of glass. He had also given us two cut-glass goblets, on one of which is Jeannie's name and my name on the other. They are very beautiful. The block, however, did not immediately impress us. It seemed to be too modern. Hence I hid it in the undergrowth for a long time until it became weather-beaten and dark and part of the earth around it. Then I placed it at the edge of the stream, and as I did so I remembered the words of the man who created it. 'I am giving you this so that there will be a memorial to the two words that mean so much to so many people: MONTY'S LEAP.'

I arrived at the solitude gate, reaching it after walking up the lane under a canopy of elm tree branches, bright green again after recovering from the decimation of the elm disease. I rested my arms on the top of the gate, akimbo, farmer fashion and talked to the donkeys. As I did so I saw the figure of a young woman coming down the field from the direction of blackthorn alley. I continued to talk to the donkeys. They were in lugubrious mood.

'Cheer up,' I said. 'Just remember what donkeys all over the world have to put up with.'

I had no biscuits to give them, no carrots.

'Come on,' I said, 'you give pleasure to so many people who come here that you can spare a bit of pleasure for me.' Then I added: 'This is a test that you can show me real love, not cupboard love.'

Susie moved forward, the black cross on her grey back dazzlingly clear.

'What about you?' I asked Merlin, and he too moved forward. I was nuzzling both of them when the young woman reached us. She was in floods of tears.

She had come to Minack before with a young family from London. They had seemed to be a happy family, although I remember having a certain reservation. The woman was much more enthusiastic about being at Minack than her husband. He was distant.

When someone is in tears it is best to ignore the tears unless they are prolonged. Then comes the moment when one has to break into the private grief, whatever it may be. So it was in this case. The tears, and the sobs, were prolonged.

213

'Tell me,' I said, trying to remember her name, 'what is so upsetting you?'

The donkeys were looking at her, experienced eyes totting up the possibility that she had the key to their cupboard love. A minute passed, and they came to the conclusion she had no key; they drifted away into the field.

'What's upsetting you?' I repeated.

'My husband has left me' – and there was another burst of tears – 'just left me suddenly. He set off after breakfast to go to his office, said goodbye to me and the two children, and never came back. Then the next day a letter came saying our marriage was over.'

I was not going to ask about the whys and wherefores. I just put my arm around her shoulders and asked: 'How is it that you are here?'

'I drove here overnight,' she replied. 'I didn't think you would mind. I wanted to feel the comfort of Minack. I have been so happy here . . . the visits and the books, both. I feel it is a kind of home. You don't mind, do you? You understand?'

All over the world there are heartbreaks every moment.

'Of course I understand. Yes, feel at home. Wander where you will.' Then, trying to stop her tears, I said: 'I have an idea. I am in Merlin and Susie's black books because I've brought them neither biscuits nor carrots. Would you like to do something for me and for them?'

'What's that?' she asked, and curiosity was stemming the tears.

'Well,' I said, 'you can move faster than I can. Would you run to the cottage and collect from the back

214

of the Volvo a packet of biscuits and a handful of carrots which are there?'

She set off at a run and soon returned. The donkeys were no longer lugubrious, nor was the young woman. She began to laugh as she teased Susie with a carrot.

I took her back to the cottage and gave her bread and cheese and a glass of wine, and I listened to her sadness. There was nothing I could say or do except to listen. Then she said goodbye, adding that she wanted to go once more to the Ambrose Rock and sit there, and find a strength that would propel her future.

'I feel much better. I *knew* that Minack would help me.'

That evening, after a still day, the wind began to murmur. Gently at first, rising to sudden gusts. The rain arrived soon after dusk. I was sitting on the sofa, ruminating, and I had been honoured by Cherry sitting on my lap. As always there was a price to pay for such an honour. I would have liked a drink, and I could not fetch it.

At first the rain pattered softly on the roof then, in an instant, it became a crescendo and peppered the roof, sounding like the rattle of ceremonial drums.

It became soft again, as if it was caressing the roof, then back again with another rattle of drums.

The rain served as a curtain around me, holding memories of Jeannie, keeping at bay imaginary anxieties, remembering happy moments, exciting me with optimism for the future . . . and always protecting the escape route for those, like the young woman today, who believe they can find a peace for themselves at Minack, in mind or in reality.

XIV

The cherry tree never flowered that summer. An easterly gale blew the petals away at the beginning of May; and, for the first time since Jeannie found Cherry at the base of the cherry tree, the branches were bare. A fey person like Jeannie might have had a twinge of apprehension. I took the loss in my stride.

At the beginning of September Cherry developed an exceptional appetite. I thought it might be a worm problem, and I asked the vet to come out and give an opinion. He was reassuring, but to be on the safe side he gave me some pills for her. Everything else about her seemed normal, including her energy. One morning she climbed to the top of the massive chimney where the Lager Louts like to squat and bellow. She liked to behave like an acrobat, jumping from table to table; and when a visitor asked what age she was, I would reply by saying, 'She behaves like a kitten.'

It was early October that I had my own first twinge of apprehension. When, as a stray, she first arrived at Minack, she had to compete with Ambrose. She would avoid him by entering the cottage through the bathroom window . . . and then she would treat the bathroom as her personal home, using the little cupboard as her personal sleeping hideout. Sometimes I would find her there just sitting, contemplating. At other times I would find her curled in the little cupboard. She had long given up this routine, but now, at the beginning of October she had taken it up again. She would be in the bathroom for hour after hour. I thought it strange, and instinct told me to ask for the vet to check her again.

He seemed worried, and said she had lost weight since he had last seen her. He said he would give her an antibiotic injection which would make her sleepy, and would continue to have an effect on her for two days. He gave her the injection and to my pleasure she decided to forsake the bathroom and make my bed her sleeping quarters. Thus all night I could stretch out my hand and touch her.

At lunchtime the next day – it was a Wednesday – the vet came out again. He was such a conscientious person. This time after examining her he said that she was becoming very weak. He gave her a pill, and she struggled so violently as he put it in her mouth that I said, 'She doesn't behave as if she is very weak.'

When the vet had gone, Cherry returned to the bathroom and the cupboard. All the afternoon and into the evening I stayed with this little cat who had never caught a bird in her life. I lay on the floor beside her, stroking her, asked for a purr and got one. I lay there thinking that I would never know where she came from or who was the first to see her as a kitten. I would never know how she made the journey to isolated Minack. I would never know what made her curl up beneath the cherry tree where Jeannie found her. It was a sad vigil.

Then, at about ten o'clock, she suddenly perked up, and she stared at me with eyes so bright that I could not believe she was ill. Her eyes were telling me something. I had an uncanny awareness that she was desperately wanting me to understand the message she was trying to give me.

And I did understand.

The message was this: 'No longer need you worry what would happen to me if something happened to you.'

Out of the stillness of the night I heard Jeannie's voice:

> The Spirits of Minack
> Welcome you
> To their
> World of Forever
> Where life continues
> And death is never.